# GUN CRIMES

2012

Titles in the True Forensic Crime Stories series:

## BONES
### DEAD PEOPLE DO TELL TALES
Library Ed. ISBN 978-0-7660-3669-7
Paperback ISBN 978-1-59845-363-8

## CYBERCRIME
### DATA TRAILS DO TELL TALES
Library Ed. ISBN 978-0-7660-3668-0
Paperback ISBN 978-1-59845-361-4

## DNA AND BLOOD
### DEAD PEOPLE DO TELL TALES
Library Ed. ISBN 978-0-7660-3667-3
Paperback ISBN 978-1-59845-362-1

## FINGERPRINTS
### DEAD PEOPLE DO TELL TALES
Library Ed. ISBN 978-0-7660-3689-5
Paperback ISBN 978-1-59845-364-5

## GUN CRIMES
### DEAD PEOPLE DO TELL TALES
Library Ed. ISBN 978-0-7660-3763-2
Paperback ISBN 978-1-59845-365-2

## TRACE EVIDENCE
### DEAD PEOPLE DO TELL TALES
Library Ed. ISBN 978-0-7660-3664-2
Paperback ISBN 978-1-59845-366-9

# GUN CRIMES

**TRUE** forensic **CRIME** stories

## Dead People Do Tell tales

**Michelle Faulk, PhD**

**Enslow Publishers, Inc.**
40 Industrial Road
Box 398
Berkeley Heights, NJ 07922
USA

http://www.enslow.com

Faulk, Michelle.
 Gun crimes : dead people do tell tales / Michelle Faulk.
  p. cm. — (True forensic crime stories)
 Includes bibliographical references and index.
 Summary: "Learn about ballistics by reading about real cases, and find out about careers in the field"
—Provided by publisher.
 ISBN 978-0-7660-3763-2
 1. Forensic ballistics—Case studies—Juvenile literature. 2. Criminal investigation—Case studies
—Juvenile literature. 3. Forensic sciences—Case studies—Juvenile literature. I. Title.
 HV8077.F38 2012
 363.25'62—dc22
                            2010039475
Paperback ISBN 978-1-59845-365-2

Printed in China

052011 Leo Paper Group, Heshan City, Guangdong, China

10 9 8 7 6 5 4 3 2 1

**To Our Readers:** We have done our best to make sure all Internet Addresses in this book were active
and appropriate when we went to press. However, the author and the publisher have no control over
and assume no liability for the material available on those Internet sites or on other Web sites they
may link to. Any comments or suggestions can be sent by e-mail to comments@enslow.com or to the
address on the back cover.

**Photo Credits:** Associated Press, pp. 8, 9, 17, 48, 50, 60–61, 63, 79, 85, 86; www.firearmsid.com,
pp. 66, 67 (top three); © GEOATLAS, p. 6; Getty Images: © Archive Photos, p. 25, © Gamma-
Keystone, p. 19, © New York Daily News, pp. 40, 73, © Photographer's Choice, p. 10, © Time &
Life Pictures, p. 51; MedicImage RF/Photolibrary, p. 13; Photo Researchers, Inc.: New York Public
Library, pp. 38–39, Philippe Psaila, p. 34, Ted Kinsman, p. 67 (hollow-point mushroom);
Shutterstock.com, pp. 1, 3, 5, 22, 24, 56, 68, 81, 88.

**Cover Photo:** Shutterstock.com

# Contents

Bosnia-Herzegovina, Croatia, Serbia, Montenegro, Slovenia, and Macedonia had been independent countries before World War I. Then they became states within the country of Yugoslavia.

# War Crimes in Croatia

Imagine yourself visiting a hospital. A few miles away there is a farm. You might picture helpful doctors and nurses, patients, as well as open fields and farmers. You would most likely not think of terrorized civilians, executions, and mass graves . . . unless you had been in Yugoslavia in 1991.

After World War I, the country of Yugoslavia was created in Europe. The victorious allied powers combined the countries of Bosnia-Herzegovina, Croatia, Serbia, Montenegro, Slovenia, and Macedonia. These previously independent countries were now states within the new country of Yugoslavia. Each one had a very different culture and religion. Now they were expected to live together peacefully under one flag. The plan ultimately failed.

In 1991, Croatia declared its independence from Yugoslavia. At this time the leader of Yugoslavia was Slobodan Milosevic, a Serb. Because many Serbs lived in Croatia, he wanted this state brought back under his power. For this reason, the Yugoslavian government backed the state of Serbia when it declared war on Croatia.

In July of 1991, Serbian forces invaded Croatia. The small town of Vukovar became a battlefield for eighty-six days. On November 18, when the fall of Vukovar seemed certain, the warring governments came to an agreement on how to humanely treat captives. Vukovar fell to the Serbs on November 19. Croatian civilians and soldiers took refuge in the town's hospital. They waited to be safely evacuated. The Serbian army had been given orders to take no revenge on their captives. They ignored these orders.

As soon as the fighting was over, people tried to enter the city to help the captive Croatians. A man named Cyrus Vance was a United Nations peace mediator at this time. It was his job to see that captives were not treated inhumanely. The International Red Cross was also present with medicine for the many people injured during the fighting. When Vance's team and the Red Cross tried to enter Vukovar, they were stopped. The group was accompanied by reporter Ian Traynor of Britain's *Guardian* newspaper. Traynor reported that Major Veselin Sljivancanin of the Serbian army prevented these people from entering the city. He stalled by telling them it was unsafe for them to proceed. Vance was

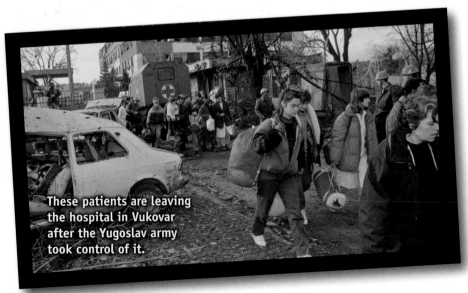

These patients are leaving the hospital in Vukovar after the Yugoslav army took control of it.

These remains are believed to be mostly Croatian civilians and soldiers killed during the siege of Vukovar.

a kind and calm gentleman, but he became very angry at being prevented from helping the Croatian people. "Nonsense. I demand access to that hospital. Stop blocking our way," he yelled. Vances's efforts were in vain and he never reached the Croatian captives in time to protect them.[1]

While Vance and the Red Cross were kept out of the city, armed Serbs searched the streets of Vukovar and shot people. At the hospital the men and women were separated. The Serbian military beat the Croatian captives. Eventually, nearly all of the people in the hospital were forced onto buses and taken to a pig farm in Ovcara, four kilometers away from Vukovar. They included Croatian soldiers, hospital staff, and civilians.

Dragutin Glasnovic was one captive being taken to the pig farm at Ovcara. He said, "I met Sljivancanin in Ovcara, and he shouted at us that we were war criminals. Sljivancanin didn't take into account

# BULLET BASICS

An unfired piece of ammunition is called a **cartridge**, or a **round**. All ammunition for handguns and **rifles** have similar parts.

1. The **bullet** itself is the projectile that is shot out of the gun. It is usually made of lead.

2. **Gunpowder** is made of chemicals that burn quickly and create expanding gases. The gases are what push the bullet out of the gun.

3. The **primer** is a small amount of explosive chemicals that ignite the gunpowder. A common primer mixture includes lead styphnate, antimony sulfide, barium nitrate, and other chemicals.

4. The cartridge case, or **shell**, is a metal case that surrounds the primer, the gunpowder, and the bullet. The shell stays behind in the gun after the bullet has been fired.

5. Some shells have a rim to hold them securely in the gun.

Cartridges are described by their **caliber**. The caliber of ammunition describes its diameter. A .38-caliber cartridge is 0.38 inches in diameter and a 9mm cartridge is 9 millimeters in diameter.

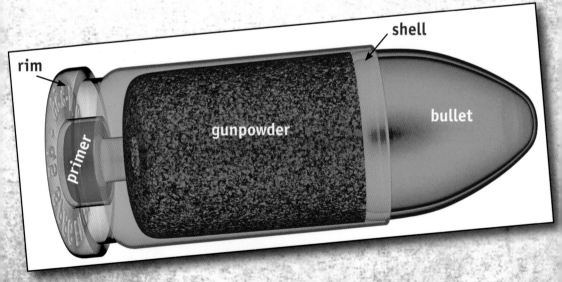

shell

rim

primer

gunpowder

bullet

that there were civilians among us—women, children, and old people. He behaved in the most awful and inhumane manner."[2]

At the farm in Ovcara there were more beatings and torture. People were once again loaded onto buses and driven to a spot about a mile from the farm. The prisoners at the farm kept hoping that they would be rescued. But the buses kept returning empty, only to load more captives. Hundreds of people who had lived in Vukovar during the fighting were never seen again.

Were hundreds of Vukovar captives really murdered at the farm in Ovcara by the Serbian military? The science of **firearms identification** would help answer this question.

## HOW A GUN FIRES A BULLET

Every gun uses the same basic steps when firing a bullet:

1. A cartridge is loaded into the gun. As the trigger of the gun is pulled back, the hammer, which contains a **firing pin**, is cocked.

2. When the trigger is fully pulled, the hammer is released and shoots forward. The hammer drives the firing pin into the primer cap.

3. When struck with the firing pin, the primer chemicals create heat and gases and a small explosion occurs. The flame from the exploded primer then ignites the gunpowder and high pressure gases are created.

4. The gases force the bullet out of the cartridge and down the barrel of the gun. The rifling of the barrel spins the bullet as it leaves the gun and the escaping gases make a "bang."

## What Is Firearms Identification?

Firearms identification is part of the larger field of forensic science. (Firearms identification is often, but incorrectly, called **ballistics**.) The main goal of firearms identification is to solve crimes committed with guns. The people who conduct these investigations are called **firearms investigators**. The firearms investigators microscopically examine bullets and cartridge shells fired from guns during a crime. They also examine guns suspected of being used in crimes. Firearms investigators can identify the caliber and manufacturer of the ammunition (ammo) used as well as determine the manufacturer of the firearm used. Firearms investigators also test fire suspected guns to see if they match bullets and shells found at a crime scene. Most importantly, firearms investigators testify in court concerning their findings.

How do firearms investigators determine the type of ammo or the kind of gun used in a crime? They do this by examining identifying marks left on bullets and cartridge shells. The metals used to make bullets and cartridge shells are softer than the metal used to make gun parts. This means that every time a gun is fired, the working parts of the gun leave unique marks on the bullets and shells.

Probably the most important marks left by a gun on bullets and shells are **rifling** marks and **striations**. When a gun barrel is made, hard metal tools create rifling grooves. Scratches or bumps on the rifling tool will leave unique marks inside each gun barrel. The marks inside the gun barrel then make unique marks on bullets and shells. Even firearms of the same make and model will produce different and distinctive marks on fired bullets and shell casings.

## The Investigation of the Vukovar Massacre

Did mass exterminations of Croatian citizens and soldiers really occur? After the war ended, what looked like mass graves were found near

# RIFLING AND STRIATIONS

This bullet is being scanned for marks to help identify the gun it came from.

It was discovered hundreds of years ago that cutting spiral **grooves** into the inside of the barrel of a gun would cause the bullets to spin and fly straighter. It is the same reason football players put a spin on the ball when they throw it. The process of cutting these grooves into a gun barrel is called *rifling*.

The metal tools used to cut the rifling grooves inside a gun barrel are very hard. However, they still get worn down a little bit each time they are used. This means that each gun barrel that is rifled with that tool will have different marks inside it. As a result, every gun barrel is unique. The raised parts in between the grooves are called **lands**. When a bullet is pushed through a gun's barrel, the raised lands leave marks on the bullet. Rifling marks on a bullet tell investigators the number of lands and grooves, their width, and whether they have a left or right twist. This information can identify the make and model of the gun.

Other marks left on a bullet are necessary to tell if a specific gun fired a certain bullet. The more a gun is fired, the more scratches build up inside the barrel. There may also be rust or dirt in the barrel that will mark a bullet or shell. These small marks are called *striations*. Other parts of the gun like the firing pin, breech face, extractor, and ejector can leave identifying marks on the shell casing. Firearms investigators test fire guns and compare the marks on the test bullets and shells to ones from a crime scene.

the Ovcara pig farm outside Vukovar. Beginning in 1992, a United Nations Commission of Experts performed archaeological excavations to determine if these were indeed mass graves. Many people within the Yugoslavian government did not want this investigation to take place, and ultimately only one grave was examined. It was declared a mass grave because it contained approximately two hundred bodies. Because the grave was in such an isolated area it suggested the deaths were meant to be secret and undiscovered. Skeletons were found with gunshot wounds to the back of the head, indicating execution-style killings. Two bodies had necklaces with Roman Catholic crosses and one was engraved "God and Croatians" on it. This evidence indicated the grave contained the bodies of Croatians. There was strong evidence of a massacre.

Many members of the Yugoslav/Serb military were brought up on charges of war crimes. Even Yugoslavian president Slobodan Milosevic was charged. At a trial held in Belgrade, Serbia, more evidence was given to show that innocent people had been mass murdered.[3] Professor Davor Strinović, a forensic medicine specialist at the Institute for Forensic Medicine at the University of Zagreb, performed examinations of the corpses from one of the graves. Dr. Strinović identified 192 of the 200 bodies using information from family members who were seeking missing persons, examining personal items found with the bodies, and using DNA analysis. All of these people were verified as having been in Vukovar during the battle before they went missing.

It had now been proven that a massacre took place, but was the Yugoslav/Serb military responsible? At the war crimes trial, Professor Miloš Tasić, a forensic medicine specialist at the University of Novi Sad, testified. He had also examined the bodies removed from the grave. Based on what Dr. Tasić had found, a number of conclusions could be made. Two of the bodies he examined were of women and one may have been pregnant. This further proved that civilians had been killed.

One hundred and ninety-two of the bodies had gunshot wounds that went right through them. This indicated that powerful firearms had been used. Because 540 bullets had been found in and around the bodies, this indicated that automatic weapons had been used. These are weapons that fire many bullets very quickly. Finally, thirty-two of the bodies had been shot in the back of the head. This indicated execution-style killings. The evidence of fully automatic weapons, high-powered ammunition, and execution-style killings suggested that the military was guilty of these deaths. But more solid evidence was needed.

Firearms identification methods helped to clearly establish that military weapons were used in these murders.[4] Four hundred and thirty-five shell casings were collected from the grave at the Ovcara farm. These were sent to the United States Bureau of Alcohol, Tobacco and Firearms (ATF) laboratory in Maryland. It was there that firearms investigators determined that all of the shells had come from AK-47 assault rifles— the same rifles used by the Yugoslav/Serb army. Also, by examining the marks on these shells, ATF firearms investigators determined that eighteen separate guns had been used in the killings. Two survivors who testified at the War Crimes Tribunal said that there were eighteen gunmen. There was now evidence that clearly showed that the military forces that invaded Vukovar had taken revenge on the Croatian people. They had murdered them in a field and then buried them in hidden mass graves. Many members of the military and government were sent to jail, including Milosevic.

While war crimes continue to occur all over the globe, at least the United States was able to assist the small country of Croatia. The evidence gathered using the ATF's state-of-the-art firearms identification methods helped bring closure to victims' families by bringing war criminals to justice.

## 2

# The St. Valentine's Day Massacre

I n the 1920s, America was deep in the era of Prohibition. All alcoholic beverages had been outlawed. Some people felt the government shouldn't have the right to tell its citizens what to drink, so they bought illegal liquor. Many organized crime gangs were bootleggers who supplied the illegal liquor and made a huge profit at the same time. The city of Chicago was a hotbed of bootlegging. While there was plenty of money to go around, competition between the crime gangs led to death and mayhem.

## The Massacre

It was the morning of February 14, 1929. Seven men were gathered in the dingy S.M.C. Cartage Co.'s garage on North Clark Street in Chicago. Adam Heyer, James Clark, Pete and Frank Gusenberg, and Albert Weinshank were active members of George "Bugs" Moran's gang. Johnny May was a former safe blower who now worked as a mechanic for Bugs.

Dr. Reinhardt Schwimmer was an optometrist. He found it very exciting to hang out with these criminals and then brag to his friends. But today was a bad day to be hanging out with Bugs' gang.

At approximately 10:00 A.M., a car pulled up in front of the garage and parked. It looked like a cop car because big black Cadillacs were often used by the Chicago police. Witness accounts are a little sketchy, but at least four men got out of the car. Two of the men wore Chicago police department uniforms while the other men were dressed in street clothes. The men made a beeline for the garage and entered with hand-guns drawn. The seven men in the garage did not resist as they were lined up next to one another facing a brick wall. The men in street clothes and police uniforms opened fire and shot the men until the room was filled with smoke. They used machine guns and a **shotgun** to do their gruesome work. When they were finished, the bodies of the seven men lay piled upon one another.

Al Capone was a gangster who was suspected of having some involvement in the St. Valentine's Day Massacre.

When the shooters left the building, the men in street clothes went out first with their hands up. The men in uniform followed behind them with their guns drawn. To many witnesses it looked like criminals were being arrested after a shootout. The black Cadillac casually pulled away from the garage but then soon floored it out of the area. Because the garage's dog, Highball, was barking horribly from the noise of the executions, neighbors began to gather. One brave soul entered the garage, but the sight of seven bloodied dead men was all he needed to see. He ran and called the police.

Police sergeant Thomas J. Loftus was the first on the scene. What he saw turned the stomach of even this thirty-eight-year veteran police officer. Amazingly, Frank Gusenberg was still alive despite being shot fourteen times. Officer Loftus spoke to Frank, who recognized the police officer. Loftus tried to get some information from the dying man about what had happened. Frank told Officer Loftus, "I won't talk."[1] Frank Gusenberg died shortly after arriving at the hospital.

## Dr. Calvin Goddard and the Evidence

The police called in coroner Dr. Herman N. Bundesen, who did a meticulous job of handling the crime scene. First, he ordered that nothing be moved. Second, he had a photographer take many pictures of the entire scene, inside and out, and from all different angles. Third, he made sure that all empty shells, bullets, and bullet fragments were collected with care. These crucial pieces of evidence were sealed inside marked envelopes. The envelopes were lined with fabric so that the evidence would not be scratched. Bullets and bullet fragments removed from the bodies were also placed in marked envelopes. A lot of crime scenes at this time were not handled with so much care. Dr. Bundesen was ahead of his time.

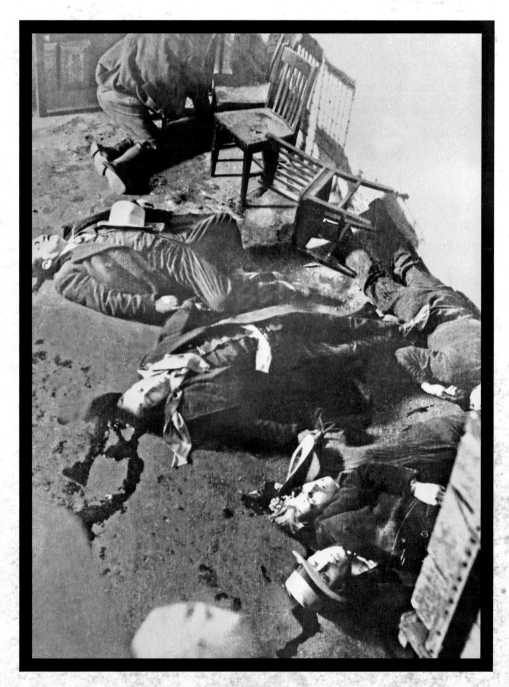

The St. Valentine's Day Massacre happened on Valentine's Day, 1929.

Dr. Bundesen chose a group of the most educated and prominent men in the community to be the jury that would review the evidence. The foreman of the jury, Mr. Massee, decided that a reliable expert in firearms identification was needed. After some investigating, Mr. Massee came across forensic scientist Dr. Calvin Goddard. When Goddard arrived in Chicago, he was a little shocked but delighted when he was handed the largest number of crime scene bullets and shell casings he had ever worked with. Goddard was extremely thorough in examining the evidence in this case. Later he published a paper detailing his very careful investigation and it was used as a guide for firearms investigators everywhere.[2]

To begin, Goddard separated and organized all the evidence. To make the most careful examinations of the evidence as he could, he photographed each piece and enlarged the prints. This method allowed even the smallest details to be magnified and compared.

Next, Goddard examined the shell casings that had been scattered about on the floor of the Clark Street Garage. Seventy .45-caliber pistol shell casings had been collected by police. All were made by the United States Cartridge Company. The first question Goddard asked himself was whether these shells came from a .45-caliber **revolver**, a **semiautomatic**, or an automatic gun.

Goddard used logic to answer the question. Witness statements said the shooting lasted for less than a minute. In that short amount of time, many bullets were fired. This indicated to Goddard that fully automatic weapons had been used. Revolvers have to be unloaded and loaded by hand, and that would have taken too long. Semiautomatic guns are faster and hold more bullets than revolvers, but even they didn't seem fast enough to create a crime scene like this. When Goddard examined the shells he found that all of them had ejector and extractor marks. Only semiautomatic or automatic guns would make these marks on a shell.

Furthermore, because the ejector and extractor marks on all of the shells were so similar, Goddard knew that all the shells came from the same make of gun. *Which* make of gun was the next question.

At this time, there were three weapons that used .45-caliber pistol cartridges: a .45-caliber Colt automatic pistol, a .45-caliber Savage Arms automatic pistol, and a .45-caliber Colt Thompson submachine gun. The Thompson was called a submachine gun because it used pistol cartridges instead of **rifle** ammo. When bullets are fired from the Colt and Savage pistols, the shells are not pushed back into the **breech face** as hard as they are in a Thompson submachine gun. The marks observed on all of the shells were very deep. This indicated that all seventy shells were fired from Thompson

# FIREARMS IDENTIFICATION AND BALLISTICS

The terms "firearms identification" and "ballistics" are often used to describe the forensic science methods used to investigate gun crimes. Dr. Calvin Goddard, one of the founding fathers of forensic firearms identification, wanted to come up with a shorthand term for this field of science. After all, "forensic firearms identification" can be a mouthful. Goddard decided "ballistics" would be a good choice. Goddard understood that ballistics is technically the study of how a projectile moves through the air and into a target. While a bullet leaving a gun is a projectile, the science of forensic firearms identification includes much more than just tracing the path of a bullet. But again, this was supposed to be just a nickname among the scientists. Unfortunately, the term "ballistics" became so popular it nearly replaced the proper name in many people's minds. Goddard then regretted having begun the trend. Goddard was quoted in 1953, "From that day onward, scientific identification of firearms has popularly been known as ballistics, and the more I struggle to correct the trend that I so innocently started, the wider the usage becomes."[3]

**semi-automatic pistol**

**revolver**

submachine guns. Now Goddard needed to know how many Thompson submachine guns had been used in the killings.

Goddard looked closer at the ejector marks left on the seventy shell casings and found that there were two different types. Twenty of the shells had one straight line with even parallel lines coming up from it at a right angle. Fifty of the shells had one wavy line with other wavy lines coming up from it. These two different ejector marks indicated that two different Thompson submachine guns had been used at the crime scene.

The bullets were next. Thirty-nine whole bullets and fragments were taken from the dead bodies during their autopsies, but only nine were intact enough to be studied. Fourteen .45-caliber

## REVOLVERS AND SEMIAUTOMATICS

The reason that the majority of crimes are committed with handguns is because they are small and easy to conceal. There are two main types of handguns. A revolver has a **cylinder** that swings out from the gun and holds five to six bullets. Pulling the trigger rotates the cylinder, cocks the hammer, and then releases it so the firing pin hits the primer of the cartridge. The cylinder has to be opened to remove empty shells and to load new ammo. The second type of handguns are automatic and semiautomatic pistols. The bullets in these guns are loaded into a **magazine** that is snapped into the handle of the gun. A magazine can hold fifteen to nineteen cartridges. These pistols have a **slide** that covers the barrel. When a bullet is fired, the force of the explosion propels both the empty shell and the slide backwards. Pushing the slide back cocks the hammer, making the gun ready to fire again. The shell goes backwards until it is stopped by the **ejector**. Then the **extractor** arm tilts the shell, allowing it to pop out of the gun. Semiautomatics fire one bullet each time the trigger is pulled. A fully automatic gun continues to fire until the trigger is released. This type of gun is usually in the form of an assault rifle. It is difficult for U.S. citizens to get the special permits needed to buy fully automatic guns.

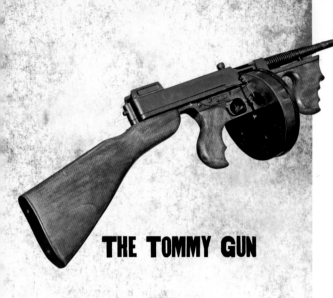

# THE TOMMY GUN

John Taliaferro Thompson invented the Thompson submachine gun. He first became interested in firearms in the army. When he retired in 1914, he set out to develop an automatic rifle. He believed that a weapon between a pistol and a rifle would be valuable for the military. He eventually came up with a gun that feeds large amounts of ammunition from a drum magazine, has two grips so it is held with both hands, and has a very short butt. Thompson called it the submachine gun but the catchier name of "Tommy gun" became more popular. Because this gun is fully automatic, it continues to fire bullets nonstop until the trigger is released. There are many types of automatic weapons available, even pistols. In the U.S. today it is very difficult for citizens to own automatics because they require special permits that are hard to get.

automatic bullets had also been collected from inside the garage. Twelve of these bullets were too damaged by traveling through bodies and hitting the brick walls to be of any use. The other two bullets were in good enough condition to give clues. This gave Goddard a total of eleven intact bullets to examine. Goddard found that all eleven of these bullets had a small letter "s" stamped on them. This indicated that they had been made by the U.S. Cartridge Company. All eleven bullets had the same rifling pattern of six grooves with a right twist. There were three guns at the time with this type of rifling: a Smith & Wesson 1917 revolver, a .45-caliber Savage Arms automatic pistol, and a .45-caliber Colt Thompson submachine gun. Now both the shell casings and the bullets told Goddard that a Thompson submachine gun had been used. To make extra sure, Goddard obtained new .45-caliber ammunition from the U.S. Cartridge Company and fired these bullets through all three types of guns. The rifling on the crime scene bullets definitely matched those of the Thompson submachine gun.

## Were the Police Involved?

Goddard's detailed examination of the evidence determined that the seven men shot in the Clark Street garage were killed with two Thompson submachine guns. The problem now was finding out if the police were involved. The police department denied the accusations, but it was

Investigators examine evidence from a Moran Gang shooting.
The man on the left is holding a Tommy Gun.

well known that corruption was rampant in Chicago. The papers had gotten hold of the story and the stories of killer cops had the public up in arms.[4] The killers had dressed and acted like Chicago police in front of witnesses and it was up to Goddard to figure out if this was just a trick. To answer this question, Goddard tested all eight of the Thompson submachine guns that the Chicago police had in their possession. He test fired the same type of ammunition through each one into cotton. Each bullet and shell casing was numbered in order. When Goddard compared these bullets and casings to those from the crime scene he found no matches. This did not mean that he had proved the police were not involved in the massacre. It just meant that Goddard had found no evidence that pointed a finger at the police. But Goddard's analysis did calm the public and moved the investigation in other directions.

## Was Al Capone Responsible?

Some time had passed since the shootings and no one had been arrested. Citizens were getting angry and a $100,000 reward was even offered. Chicago was tired of living in fear of criminals. Police were under a lot of pressure to do something about it. Gangster Al Capone was an important player in the Chicago crime scene. He and his gang had committed many crimes, but Capone had managed to stay out of prison. In this case, Capone had a strong alibi. At the time of the murders he was being questioned by police in Florida. But he and his gang remained under suspicion and the police continued their investigations.

One Capone gang member that police suspected was involved in the massacre was Jack McGurn. He was a well known executioner for Al Capone. McGurn also had an alibi for the time of the massacre. He said he was with a woman named Louise Rolfe. Rolfe backed up McGurn's story and became known as the Blond Alibi. McGurn got off.

The police still had other suspects, such as John Scalise, Albert Anselmi, and Joseph "Hop Toad" Guinta. All three of these men were arrested but all three made bail. Before any of the men could be tried in a court of law they were dead. They were found by police in Indiana. Two were lying down in the back of a car with the third lying on the ground.[5] All three had been very badly beaten and shot. There have been many theories about what happened to Scalise, Anselmi, and Guinta. One of the more frequently told stories is that Capone suspected these men of being traitors.[6] He laid a trap and had another man named Frankie Rio pretend to befriend them to get information. After Rio told Capone that the three men could not be trusted, Capone threw them a party. By the end of the party, all three men had been shot. While it is a good story, exactly how Scalise, Anselmi, and Guinta were murdered may never be known.

The big break in the case came on December 14, 1929, in Michigan. Two men had a car accident in front of a police station. A small argument started but one man decided he wasn't going to stick around. This man was Fred "Killer" Burke, who was wanted by the Chicago police for questioning in the St. Valentine's Day Massacre. Police officer Charles Skelly had witnessed the accident and jumped on the running board of the other man's car. A chase began. After only a short time Burke stopped his car and got out. As Officer Skelly approached him, Burke pulled a .45-caliber automatic pistol and shot Skelly three times, killing him. Burke then took off again. Later, Burke's car was found abandoned. When police searched the car they found information that led them to Burke's home. When police searched the house they hit the jackpot. They found two Thompson submachine guns, rifles, shotguns, revolvers, and a lot of ammunition.

The two machine guns and ammunition were immediately sent from Michigan to Dr. Goddard for examination. First, Goddard found that the ammunition from Burke's home was the same type as that used in the murders. The ammo was made by the U.S. Cartridge Co. and a small "s" was stamped on each one. Goddard then test fired this ammunition in the two confiscated guns. Goddard determined that the bullet taken from Reinhardt Schwimmer's body was fired from one of these guns, and one bullet taken from James Clark's body was fired from the other gun. There was no doubt that these two guns were used in the St. Valentine's Day Massacre. On December 23, 1929, Dr. Calvin Goddard testified before the Coroner's Jury in Chicago. He presented evidence that the machine guns used in the murders committed at 2122 North Clark Street were the ones found in the house of Fred Burke. Because of Goddard's objective and careful examination of the evidence, Fred Burke was charged with murder. However, it was never determined whether Burke had been one of the shooters in the St. Valentine's Day Massacre because he never made it to Chicago to be tried in court. Michigan kept Burke and found him guilty of murdering Officer Skelly. He served a life sentence in that state.

Despite the great work of Dr. Calvin Goddard and the Chicago police, no one was ever sent to jail for the St. Valentine's Day murders. Fred Burke died in a Michigan prison. McGurn had gotten off but was machine-gunned to death in 1936. Scalise, Anselmi, and Guinta were killed and left beside an Indiana road. Finally, there was never any direct evidence that tied Capone to the murders. While the St. Valentine's Day Massacre goes down in history as one of the most vicious crimes committed, it played another important role in history. This investigation introduced to the world the basic methods for firearms identification. Dr. Calvin Goddard himself became famous, which allowed him to further improve on the methods for forensic crime investigation. While the tools have become more sophisticated, the techniques Goddard used in this case became the standard for crime scene analysis at that time.

# Firearms Experts, Real and Fake

**C**rimes committed with guns are often solved by the men and women who train to become firearms identification experts. Their work is not finished once an investigation is completed and a suspect has been arrested. These experts testify in court and explain the complicated evidence that has been gathered. It is crucial that these experts clearly and thoroughly explain their evidence to juries. Without an educated jury, justice cannot be achieved.

In the early days of firearms identification, there were few experts available to help police solve crimes and to testify in court. To make matters worse, there were many people pretending to be firearms experts just to get money or attention. One of the most infamous of these frauds was Albert Hamilton. Unfortunately, he inserted himself into two important historic cases. Fortunately, two legitimate firearms experts, Charles Waite and Calvin Goddard, were on the scene. If left to his own devices, Hamilton would have been responsible for an innocent man's execution and for setting at least one murderer free.

## Charles Stielow

Charles Stielow was a poor, uneducated German immigrant. He struggled to support his family by farming the land of a wealthy man named Charles B. Phelps. Stielow lived in a tiny house with his wife, two children, mother-in-law, and brother-in-law, Nelson Green. For Stielow, a terrifying chain of events began on a cold night in March of 1915. Gun shots rang out in the night. At daybreak, Stielow went outside to begin his chores. He was confronted with a gruesome discovery. Margaret Wolcott, Mr. Phelps' housekeeper, was lying dead in the snow near his porch steps. Her nightgown was bloody because she had been shot. Stielow made a mad dash across the road to the main farmhouse. He found the kitchen door standing wide open in the cold morning air and Charles Phelps lying on the floor. Even though the elderly man had been shot three times, he was still alive. Stielow ran to get help. Unfortunately, Phelps died shortly after.

This is where Stielow and Green's lives took a terrifying turn for the worse. Like most farmers, Stielow and Green owned guns, specifically a .22-caliber revolver and a rifle. Stielow's wife and mother-in-law were afraid these guns would draw suspicion on the family. Against his better judgment, Stielow hid the guns in the barn. Later he asked a relative to hold onto the guns for them. When Stielow and Green were questioned by the authorities in an official court hearing on March 26, they both swore that they did not own any firearms. This was a grave mistake.

After the hearing, the county authorities hired a private detective agency run by George Newton to investigate the crime. When Newton found out that Stielow and Green had lied about owning firearms, he saw these lies as evidence of guilt. Exactly what the family had been afraid of had happened; they were now suspects. To make matters worse, four bullets had been extracted from the bodies of Charles Phelps and Margaret

Wolcott. All four were .22-caliber bullets. On April 21, Newton had both Stielow and Green arrested.

While Stielow and Green were being questioned in jail, a fake firearms expert arrived in town. Albert Hamilton was a pharmacist from Auburn, New York. In 1908, he decided to become a criminalist. This was someone who examined physical evidence and was usually paid to testify at trials. He did not educate himself on forensic science, he simply published a brochure. He declared that he was an expert in the fields of handwriting analysis, photography, fingerprint analysis, and firearms identification. While he was at it, he also gave himself a medical degree.

The prosecution hired Hamilton as their firearms expert at a very high rate of $50.00 a day. After examining Stielow and Green's guns, Hamilton told detective Newton and the police that he had found nine bumps inside the barrel of Stielow's gun.[1] Hamilton also said that he had found nine scratches that matched the position of these bumps on the bullets taken from the bodies of Phelps and Wolcott. Hamilton never test fired Stielow's .22-caliber revolver, but he told police that the four bullets taken from the bodies had definitely been fired from that gun.

At this point Detective Newton, the district attorney, and the police all believed Stielow and Green were guilty. They decided a confession would seal the deal. Both men were given the "third degree" in jail, meaning that they were bullied and beaten. Stielow held out as long as he could, but after two days he just couldn't take it anymore. When the police promised that he could go home if he confessed, he did. But when the police wanted him to write down his confession he stubbornly refused. The officers finally wrote one for him but Stielow refused to sign it. These were all just details to the police. The State of New York charged Stielow and Green with first-degree murder.

Stielow went to trial before Green. Albert Hamilton gave the jury quite a show when describing his evidence. One man on the jury was doubtful and asked if they could examine the evidence and see for themselves the markings that Hamilton kept referring to. Hamilton refused the request and said that they were not educated enough to see what he saw. Despite their doubts, the jury found Stielow guilty of the two murders. He was sentenced to death and his execution date was set for April 19, 1915. To avoid the same fate, Green pleaded guilty and was sentenced to life in prison.

While Stielow was in Sing Sing prison awaiting his death, he continued to declare his innocence. The warden, Spencer Miller Jr., became convinced that this man may have been wrongly convicted. Miller made an effort to help Stielow and told other people his story. As a result, a lawyer named Grace Humiston took on Stielow's case. She began to fight for his release. A group called the Humanitarian Cult also became interested in Stielow's plight. This group of wealthy and powerful people used their social connections and money to further investigate the murders of Phelps and Wolcott. More detectives were hired and petitions were made to the authorities of New York that Stielow was innocent. Because of these efforts as well as the intense media coverage, Stielow's execution was delayed three times. One time his execution was halted only thirty minutes before he was to be killed. Finally, Governor Charles Whitman decided he should hear all the evidence for himself. Afterwards, he converted Stielow's sentence to life in prison.

An amazing thing happened next. A man named Erwin King was arrested and while in custody he confessed to the robbery of Charles Phelps.[2] King said that his partner, Clarence O'Connell, was the one who had actually shot Phelps. He also shot Margaret Wolcott as she tried to flee the house. This was encouraging news to the people supporting Stielow. Unfortunately, while in the company of the police, King suddenly and suspiciously recanted his confession. But this was only a temporary setback. It was discovered that while in jail King wrote many letters to friends. These letter contained details of the crime that only the culprit would know. These letters led the governor to reopen Stielow's case and he ordered that a new detective be hired to investigate the crime.

The man selected to head the new investigation was George H. Bond. He uncovered much evidence that supported Stielow and Green's innocence. Bond found out that:

- Stielow's confession was obtained only after Stielow was threatened and tricked.

- Stielow's confession was definitely forged since it used words that someone with Stielow's low IQ would not use.[3]

- Conversations between Stielow, Green, and their lawyers had been taped and at no time did Stielow or Green admit guilt.

- During the original investigation, Detective Newton put one of his men in jail with Stielow pretending to be another prisoner. The man befriended Stielow and had long talks with him. Stielow never once admitted guilt, never revealed any crime details, but only kept saying he was innocent.

- Finally, Erwin King made a second confession that he and Clarence O'Connell had indeed committed the murders of Phelps and Wolcott.

In addition to all of this evidence, Bond hired a real firearms expert named Charles Waite to re-examine Stielow's gun and the crime bullets. Everything that Waite discovered overturned the false evidence presented in court by Albert Hamilton. First, Waite found none of the bumps or scratches that Hamilton had mentioned. Second, Waite test fired Stielow's .22-caliber revolver by shooting bullets into cotton. He then took photographs of these bullets, along with the ones removed

Investigators sometimes test guns by shooting them into cotton. Then they can examine the marks on the bullet casing.

from the bodies, and had the images enlarged. By comparing these photographs it was obvious that the marks left by Stielow's gun barrel on the test bullets were very different from those on the crime scene bullets. This proved that Stielow's gun did not fire the bullets that killed Phelps and Wolcott.[4] Furthermore, Waite got a second opinion on the general condition of Stielow's gun from a New York City police detective known for his knowledge of firearms. Both men concluded that this gun had not been fired in a very long time.

Based on all the evidence supplied by Charles Waite and Bond's detective, Governor Whitman released both Stielow and Green from jail. Sadly, Erwin King and Clarence O'Connell were never charged with the murders of Phelps and Wolcott. The State of New York was quite embarrassed by all the news coverage of Stielow and Green being unjustly convicted. The State had also spent a great deal of money convicting and then setting free these two innocent men.[5] Since King and O'Connell were put in jail for other crimes, the New York authorities just let the matter of the murders fade away.

## Sacco and Vanzetti

Firearms identification expert Calvin Goddard played a role in one of the most controversial murder trials in American history. It all began on the afternoon of April 15, 1920, in South Braintree, Massachusetts. Frederick Parmenter and an armed guard named Alessandro Berardelli were transporting the cash payroll of the Slater & Norrill Shoe Company. They carried the $16,000 in two metal boxes. As the men walked, two other men who had been leaning on a nearby fence approached. Suddenly one of them drew a pistol from his pocket and fired several shots into Berardelli. When Parmenter saw Berardelli get shot he tried to run, but it was too late. Parmenter was also shot and died early the next morning. After the shooting, a third man appeared driving a Buick touring

# HOW TO TEST A GUN FOR EVIDENCE

When a gun arrives in a forensic firearms laboratory, the first thing that is done is to examine the inside of the barrel. When a gun fires a bullet, a "blowback" occurs. The gases that are created by the exploding gunpowder drive the bullet out of the barrel. After the bullet leaves, a small but powerful vacuum is created and anything near the barrel can be sucked in. For example, if someone is shot through a pillow in an effort to muffle the sound, fibers or feathers will almost certainly be found inside the gun's barrel. Blowback can provide investigators with important evidence about the crime.

Next, the barrel will be cleaned and the gun will be test fired. All guns are test fired twice to produce two test bullets and two test cartridge cases. A while ago this was done by firing the gun into cotton, sawdust soaked in oil, and even ten feet of phone books. Today, the FBI firearms labs use a water-filled steel tank, usually four feet wide, five feet deep, and ten feet long. The water slows the bullet down and it drops to the bottom of the tank. The water is so smooth that it does not alter any marks on the bullet or add any new ones.

car that had been parked some distance away. As the thieves were gathering up the metal boxes of money, Berardelli struggled on his hands and knees to stand up. The driver of the car saw this and jumped out and shot the man again, this time killing him. Witnesses said they saw this man take something from Berardelli before fleeing the scene. Later, investigators could not find Berardelli's .38-caliber Harrington & Richardson revolver.

As the car made its getaway through town, the men inside fired at the many witnesses on the street. No one died, but one bystander had his coat singed by a bullet that barely missed him. One of the thieves inside the car threw out handfuls of tacks to puncture the tires of anyone who attempted to chase them. The car continued speeding

through the streets of South Braintree until it vanished. Two days later and twelve miles away, the car was found abandoned in the woods near Brockton.

The next day, both bodies were autopsied. Two bullets were found in Parmenter and four were removed from Berardelli. The county medical examiner, Dr. George Burgess Magrath, was careful to keep track of each bullet as it was removed. Bullet number III turned out to be an important bullet.

- Five of the six bullets taken from the bodies had been fired from a .32-caliber pistol with a right-hand twist to the rifling. Three of these were made by the Peters Company and two by the Remington Company.

- The sixth bullet, named bullet III, was an older model bullet that was no longer made by Winchester. It had a unique groove around the edge and had been fired from a .32-caliber pistol with a left-hand twist. The gun that fired this ammo was a Colt pistol.

- Empty cartridge shells were also collected at the crime scene. Two of these were Peters, one a Remington, and one a Winchester. The Winchester was later labeled as shell W.

After interviewing witnesses, the police suspected that two of the three men involved in the April 15 murders may have been Mike Boda and Ferruccio Coacci. Coacci had been deported on April 17, so police turned their attention to Boda. They discovered that Boda had left a car to be repaired in a West Bridgewater garage. On May 5, police got a call from the garage owner that Boda and three other men—Ricardo Orciani, Nicola Sacco, and Bartolomeo Vanzetti—were at the garage. Before police could get there, Boda got suspicious and all four men left. Boda was never caught before he escaped to Italy. Orciani was eventually arrested and questioned, but released because he had an alibi for the day of the robbery. Nicola Sacco and Bartolomeo Vanzetti were also arrested after leaving the garage.

Sacco was carrying a loaded .32-caliber Colt semiautomatic. The crime scene bullets had been fired from a .32-caliber Colt pistol.[6] Both Sacco and Vanzetti had loose bullets on them. Some of them were .32-calibers made by the Peters Company and Remington, and six were out-of-date Winchesters. These were the same makes of shell casings found at the crime scene. Vanzetti was also carrying a .38-caliber Harrington and Richardson revolver. It was the same type of gun thought to be carried by Berardelli. Police believed that Sacco was the man who fired the first shots into Parmenter and Berardelli. They also believed that Vanzetti was the man who emerged from the car to finish off Berardelli.

The trial began on May 31, 1921, in Dedham, Massachusetts. The prosecution wanted to prove that the .38-caliber gun found on Vanzetti belonged to

Nicola Sacco and Bartolomeo Vanzetti were arrested for murder and robbery in 1920.

Editor  Daily News
    New York City

SACCO & VANZETTI DEATH PROTEST WARNING.

Your building and other peoples property will be destroyed this
coming week if our comrades are not set free. Therefore do all in
your power to help free them. The subway explosions are only a sample
of what will happen if our comrades are not freed. We have enough
explosives to destroy New York the poor as well as the rich will
suffer. We warn first as we did with the exploding of the bombs
in the subways,when a bomb was found last week.You and yours are
marked unless you enlist in the cause.

                    THE ANARCHISTS OF THE WORLD FOR THE
                    FREEDOM OF SACCO AND VANZETTI.

Sacco and Vanzetti had some powerful friends who sent
threatening letters to secure their release.

Berardelli. A witness to the shooting, Peter McCullum, said that one of the shooters took a "white revolver" from Berardelli's body. Berardelli's nickel-plated Harrington & Richardson revolver would have looked white in the bright sunlight. At trial, Vanzetti testified that his gun was bought from a friend named Luigi Falzini. Falzini backed up this story on the witness stand.

Vanzetti had a mixture of cartridges in his pocket when he was arrested. The make of these cartridges matched the shell casings found at the scene. Because of the bullets in his pocket, and because the jury didn't believe Falzini's testimony, Vanzetti was convicted of first-degree murder and sentenced to death.

As for Sacco, the prosecution charged that the .32-caliber Colt he was carrying when arrested was the weapon fired at Parmenter and Berardelli. The experts for the prosecution were Captain William Proctor of the Massachusetts State Police and Captain Charles Van Amburgh from the Remington Arms Company. They testified that the rifling on the test bullets matched that on the grooved Winchester bullet number III. The jury handed down a verdict of guilty of first-degree murder for Sacco and he was sentenced to death.

## Hamilton's Hijinks

At this point, things got messy. Sacco and Vanzetti's lawyers wanted a new trial and they hired fake firearms expert Albert Hamilton to re-examine the evidence. Hamilton did not perform new test fires of Sacco's gun. Instead, he examined the evidence that was already in storage using a microscope. He told the defense team that:

1. The marks on the test bullets and those on bullet III did not match, meaning bullet III had not been fired from Sacco's Colt automatic pistol.

2. The cartridge cases found at the scene and the ones in Sacco's pocket did not match.

3. None of the empty shell casings at the scene had a firing pin mark that matched Sacco's gun.

It was at this point that Hamilton outsmarted himself. He wanted to impress the judge with a dramatic demonstration. Hamilton disassembled two new .32-caliber Colt pistols along with Sacco's gun and placed all their parts in three piles on a table. He then went into a long explanation of how each part worked. When he was done, he put the guns back together, put two in his pocket, and gave Sacco's gun to the court's clerk. But as he was leaving the courtroom, Judge Thayer stopped him and demanded that the two guns in his pocket not leave the courtroom. It was later discovered that Sacco's gun had a shiny new barrel. If this gun were to be test fired now, the rifling pattern on the test bullets would definitely not match that of bullet III. The guns were given to the judge, who discovered that one of the two guns that Hamilton had used in his "demonstration" had the original barrel of Sacco's gun. It was obvious that Hamilton had switched the gun barrels to make sure that Sacco's gun could not be connected to the crime bullet or shell casings. Luckily, the judge had seen through Hamilton's dishonesty and denied the defense a new trial. Sacco and Vanzetti remained on death row, but their story was far from over.

## Dr. Calvin Goddard

Seven years after the murder of Parmenter and Berardelli, Sacco and Vanzetti were still alive, still in the news, and still trying to get out of jail. The drama of the case had captured the attention of the entire world. Many people were convinced that Sacco and Vanzetti were being blamed because they were poor immigrants. A lot of pressure was being put on Massachusetts Governor John Fuller and he finally gave in. The governor ordered that the evidence be examined a third time. Fortunately, this time a real firearms expert was there to help. Calvin Goddard was a well respected firearms expert who had been following the case closely in the press. He had studied photographs of the crime bullets that had been published in the newspapers and felt he could be of assistance in this complicated firearms identification case. He offered his services for free and both the prosecution and defense accepted his offer of help.

Goddard first did a test fire of Sacco's gun, with the original barrel in place. Using a **comparison microscope** he was able to accurately examine and compare the shell casing from the test bullet to the four empty shells found at the crime scene. He saw that marks made on the test shell casing by the gun's firing pin and breech-lock were identical to those on one of the crime scene shells (shell W). Next he examined the four bullets taken from the body of Berardelli. Goddard saw that the rifling grooves on the test bullet and bullet III were identical. They were the same depth and width, and there were additional tiny scratches on each bullet that matched perfectly. Put together, this meant that Sacco's .32-caliber Colt had been the gun that killed Berardelli.[7]

On August 23, 1927, Nicola Sacco and Bartolomeo Vanzetti were executed in the electric chair. Even so, the controversy over this case continued. As recently as 1961, firearms examiners reexamined the evidence from this case using modern firearms identification equipment.[8] It was determined that Calvin Goddard had been correct. Without a doubt it was Sacco's gun that had fired the bullets that killed guard Alessandro Berardelli. However, today it is widely accepted that Vanzetti had been innocent. Most scholars believe that the trial had more to do with Vanzetti's political connections at the time.

# THE FOUNDING FATHERS OF FIREARMS IDENTIFICATION

**Charles E. Waite** traveled the world in the 1920s cataloging the rifling (number of lands, grooves, and twists) of every gun that was mass-produced. In 1925, Waite published two articles in the *Saturday Evening Post* called "Fingerprinting Bullets."

**Dr. Calvin Goddard** went to medical school to be a heart surgeon. While in the army during World War I, he developed an interest in firearms and became a leading expert. Because of his help with the St. Valentine's Day Massacre investigation, he was hired to establish the first Scientific Crime Detection Laboratory at Northwestern University in 1929. Later, Goddard inspired and assisted J. Edgar Hoover at the FBI in opening their Criminological Laboratory in 1932.

**Philip Gravelle** was a chemist who invented the comparison microscope. This is a microscope that can hold two bullets or shells side-by-side so they can be viewed through one objective lens. Before this, investigators had to use enlarged pictures taken of bullets and shells to examine them.

**John Fisher** was a physicist who made two great contributions to forensic firearms identification. He invented the **helixometer**, which allows the inside of a gun barrel to be examined. He also developed a special microscope that allowed investigators to measure the depths of lands and grooves.

Charles Waite, Calvin Goddard, Philip Gravelle, and John Fisher joined together in 1925 to form the Bureau of Forensic Firearms Identification in New York City. Waite was head of the Bureau until he died and then Goddard took over.

# The Unpredictable Path of Bullets

No matter how straight someone shoots, once a bullet leaves a gun it may encounter bone, buttons, cement, trees, or other objects that deflect it. Cort Cunningham, a firearms examiner for the FBI, has seen first-hand the crazy routes that bullets can take. "I remember I testified in a case in Baltimore where a man sitting in a bar got into an altercation with someone else who took out a .22 and shot him right between the eyes. A police officer arrested the shooter and called the ambulance to remove the body. Halfway to the morgue the victim sat up and started complaining that he had a headache. This bullet struck his skull, went under his scalp and over the top of his head, and ended up in the back. The doctors took it out, patched him up, and he went back to the bar where the same astonished officer saw him later in the day."[1]

Stories such as these are not uncommon. In Oklahoma, a man robbed a bank and realized that a high school classmate was the teller.

Unfortunately, this man didn't want to leave any witnesses. He took the teller and other witnesses behind the building, made them kneel, and shot them. As he did with the other victims, the bank robber pressed his powerful .357 Magnum handgun into the back of the teller's head, fired, and she fell to the ground. To be sure, the robber rolled her over and saw an exit wound in the front of her head. Satisfied she was dead, he took off. Amazingly, the bullet had skidded up over her skull, traveled all the way around inside her head, and then shot out through the skin of her forehead. She did not have any brain damage and was perfectly healthy when she testified against her attacker in court.

While a powerful bullet fired into the back of a woman's head can be nearly harmless, the opposite can also occur. Take the case of a man shot with a .22-caliber bullet in the wrist. This doesn't seem like it would be a fatal wound, but the bullet just happened to hit a large vein. For some strange reason, the vein acted like a water chute. It caught the bullet's momentum and sent it up and directly into the man's heart, killing him.

Often the unpredictable behavior of bullets makes it difficult to collect them at a crime scene. During a shootout in St. Louis, Missouri, five shots were fired inside a home. One FBI agent was killed while two others were wounded. When investigators tried to reconstruct the shooting, they couldn't find the fifth bullet. Eventually it was found in the kitchen sink that was filled with water and dirty dishes. To retrace the path of this bullet, its condition, along with the damage done inside the home, was examined. The FBI firearms investigators figured out the bullet had first passed through the leg of one of the FBI agents before piercing a carpet on the kitchen floor. After hitting the floor underneath, the bullet bounced back up through the carpet where it then hit the leg of a chair, flew up against the ceiling, and finally fell down into the kitchen sink. The shooter of that bullet could never have predicted the path that bullet would take.

# RECONSTRUCTING A SHOOTING

When a shooting takes place, forensic investigators will try to reconstruct the crime scene by looking for the following clues:

- Investigators try to find every bullet and shell casing at the scene. They look for bullets in victims as well as anywhere there is a hole, like in a wall. When a shooting takes place outside, it can be very difficult to find all the bullets because they may have traveled a great distance. The number of casings found can help indicate the number of shots fired. Where the shell casings are found indicates where the shooter stood when the gun was fired.

- Tracing the path of a bullet is very difficult. Bullets rarely fly in a straight line because as soon as they hit something they will change shape and direction. Investigators like to find at least two places the bullet has been. For example, a laser beam or thin wooden rods can be inserted through two bullet holes to show the path of the bullet.

- Every gun found at a crime scene must be checked to see if it was fired, how many times, and using what bullets.

- When a bullet hits something it may get flattened. The farther a bullet travels the more it slows down. This means it will be flattened less when it finally hits something. By knowing the original length of the bullet and measuring how much it has been flattened, investigators can estimate how far the bullet traveled.

- Blood splatter patterns on and around victims may indicate what direction and angle the bullet came from.

## The Kennedy Assassination

Probably the most infamous example of how a bullet can take a bizarre path is the **assassination** of President John Fitzgerald Kennedy. It happened on November 22, 1963, in Dallas, Texas. The president, his wife Jackie, Texas Governor John Connally, and his wife Nellie rode in an open convertible through the streets, waving to onlookers. The head of the Secret Service at the White House, Roy Kellerman, rode along with them for protection.

At about 12:30 P.M., a gunshot was fired and panic broke out. The driver of the president's car braked as two more gunshots rang out.

When President John F. Kennedy (center) was shot, he was riding in a car with his wife, Jackie, and Texas Governor John Connally and his wife, Nellie (front seat).

The First Lady tried to escape the car by crawling out over the trunk. Secret Service agent Clint Hill ran to the car, pushed her back in, and shielded both her and the president with his own body. Ten seconds after the first shot was heard, the motorcade raced away from the scene to Parkland Memorial Hospital. Both President Kennedy and Governor Connally were injured. Connally had wounds to his back, chest, wrist, and thigh. The president had a severe head wound. At approximately 1:00 P.M. he was declared dead.

Vice President Lyndon Johnson was now a very important man, and the Secret Service was eager to get him out of the Dallas area. As President Kennedy's body was loaded onto Air Force One, it was decided that the vice president should take the oath of office before takeoff. Johnson, his wife Claudia "Lady Bird" Johnson, and Jackie Kennedy waited for Judge Sarah Hughes to arrive. At exactly 2:38 P.M. on November 22, Lyndon Johnson took the oath of office and became the President of the United States.

At 1:16 P.M., a Dallas police officer stopped to question a man near the crime scene. The man pulled a handgun and shot the officer, who later died. Police raced to the aid of their fellow officer and a manhunt for his killer began immediately. Johnny Brewer was in the shoe shop he managed when he noticed a man on the street who seemed to be hiding as police cars flew past. Brewer watched the man enter a nearby movie theater and called the police. Police stopped the movie and turned the lights on so Brewer could identify the man he had seen. The man did not go quietly. He attempted to shoot one of the police officers before he was wrestled to the ground. Lee Harvey Oswald was then arrested.

After intense questioning by the police, Oswald became a major suspect in the president's assassination. However, when he was being transferred to the county jail the day after the shooting, a man named Jack Ruby stepped forward from the crowd and shot Oswald in the

Lee Harvey Oswald, suspected of assassinating President Kennedy, was shot and killed by Jack Ruby.

stomach. The only suspect in the president's murder was now dead. Because the main suspect in this horrible crime could not be tried in a court, the investigation by forensic experts became even more important. The new president, Lyndon B. Johnson, appointed a seven-man commission to evaluate the evidence of the crime. This commission was led by Chief Justice Earl Warren and became known as the Warren Commission.

Three men were the primary firearms investigators in the JFK case. While the country was mourning the death of its president, these three men put their emotions away. Chief of the FBI's Firearms Unit Bob Frazier later said, "We worked exactly the same way we did in every other case, except it was decided that in this case there would be three examiners—myself, Cort Cunningham, and Charles Killion—and each of us would do his own work. All three of us came out with the same results, and those were the results that were furnished to the Warren Commission."[2]

## What Evidence Linked Oswald to the Killing?

On the day of the shooting, witnesses said they heard gunshots coming from a sixth-floor window in the Texas School Book Depository. At this window, investigators collected an empty brown paper bag, three shell casings, and a rifle that was hidden under some boxes. It was later learned that Oswald worked at the book depository and that witnesses put him

Assassin Lee Harvey Oswald's rifle, passport, and other belongings

on the sixth floor shortly before the shooting. Oswald's palm print was found on the rifle, on book cartons, and on the brown paper bag. His fingerprints were on the shell casings left behind at the scene. And although he had tried to hide it, police figured out that the gun belonged to Lee Harvey Oswald. A man using the name A. Hidell had bought the gun through the mail from Klein's Sporting Goods Company in Chicago. The handwriting on the envelope used to order the gun was later found to match Oswald's handwriting.[3] At the time of his arrest, Oswald was carrying an ID card with the name Alek Hidell. The gun had been mailed to a post office box that belonged to Oswald.

## Did Oswald's Gun Fire the Bullets that Hit the President and Governor?

As soon as the president's limousine had made its way back to Washington, the firearms investigators combed through the car looking for bullets. The men found only little bits of lead and two larger pieces of a bullet. The only complete and intact bullet investigators found was lying next to Governor Connally on his stretcher. This was the bullet that was later described as the "pristine" bullet. This became confusing because "pristine" suggests this bullet was in perfect condition, but it wasn't. It was really called pristine because it was completely intact and not fragmented. It was, however, as flat as a pancake.

The gun found in the book depository was a 6.5mm Mannlicher-Carcano Italian military rifle with one live round inside. The live round and the shell casings collected from the scene were identified as Western Cartridge Company 6.5mm cartridges. Using new ammo, the rifle was test fired into a long box filled with cotton. The test bullets had a very unique rifling pattern because something in the gun barrel made an extra deep groove in the bullets. After comparing the test bullets and shells to the bullet from the stretcher, the fragments from the car, and the shell casings from the book depository, Frazier and his team had no doubts. Oswald's gun had fired the bullets that killed President Kennedy.

## The Zapruder Film

"Trajectory" means the path a bullet takes. Firearms investigators often have to figure out trajectories to recreate a crime scene. In this investigation things were made a little easier since a man named Abraham Zapruder made a home movie of the president that captured the moments of the assassination. Frazier and his team carefully examined the Zapruder film even though it meant watching the president die over and over. They learned an important trick. The film was eight millimeters wide. But two millimeters had holes punched in it for the projector's teeth to pull the film through the machine. The images on these two

## LONG GUNS

The term "long gun" refers to **rifles and shotguns.** Compared to handguns, rifles have longer barrels and a **butt stock** (a wooden or plastic part that is held against the shoulder). Rifles are more accurate over long distances and shoot more powerful cartridges than handguns.

A shotgun does not fire bullets. Shotguns are loaded with shotgun shells that contain lead balls. These balls are called **shot.** Shotgun shells are described by their **gauge.** A 12-gauge shotgun uses lead balls that weigh 1/12 of a pound. The lower the gauge of the shotgun, the larger the balls of lead it shoots. Because shotguns do not fire cartridges, they are not rifled and are called "smooth bored."

The sale and transfer of rifles and shotguns is not as tightly regulated as handguns. Because they are easier to buy and do not involve background checks, this may make them attractive to criminals. However, a long gun is not as portable or easily hidden like a handgun. Ultimately, criminals will find a way to access illegal guns. Many are able to bypass background checks and registration requirements. This means that handguns remain the most common guns used in crimes.

millimeters don't show up when the movie runs through the projector. By photographing each individual frame, enlarging it, then laying the frames out in order, the investigators could see everything the camera caught that day. Photos and a sound recording were collected from other witnesses. These, combined with the Zapruder photos, allowed the investigators to piece together what had happened that day.

## How Many Shots Were Fired?

Three witnesses who were at the windows on the fifth floor of the book depository said they heard three shots. Investigators found three shell casings on the sixth floor of the book depository and none anywhere else. But there was a problem. People standing outside the building said they heard more than three shots. However, this made sense to investigators. The bullets flying over the heads of these people were going faster than the speed of sound. The people first heard each bullet crack the air as it went by them. Next they heard a second boom, which was the delayed sound of each bullet leaving the rifle. The hard evidence indicated that three shots were fired.

Witness statements and evidence indicated that the three shots were all fired from the sixth floor of the book depository. However, some witnesses said they heard shots coming from a grassy knoll near the book depository. Frazier and his team conducted a test in which they placed investigators in key spots and then fired a weapon from the book depository window. Some investigators confirmed they heard what seemed to be shots coming from the grassy knoll and even a few other places around the book depository. Each of these areas was thoroughly searched for evidence of a gun having been fired there. None was found. It was clear, the buildings and the hills caused an echo. The evidence supported that one man fired from the sixth-floor window of the Texas School Book Depository.

## Could Three Shots Be Fired That Fast and Still Be Accurate?

Firing accurately at a moving target is not easy. Doing it quickly is even harder. After viewing the Zapruder film, investigators estimated it could have taken the killer up to 7.9 seconds to fire three shots at the president. Firearms investigators Frazier, Cunningham, and Killion fired Oswald's gun at a firing range aiming at targets placed at fifteen yards, twenty-five yards, and one hundred yards (to simulate a moving target getting farther away). Even though they had not practiced with this gun, all three men pierced the targets within 6.5 seconds. So, Oswald could have fired the rifle three times at a moving target well within the time range established by the Zapruder film.

## How Did One Bullet Hit Both President Kennedy and Governor Connally?

The bullet that hit both men was found on Governor Connally's stretcher and is the one called the "pristine" bullet because it was not fragmented. The Zapruder film clearly shows this was the first bullet to hit the president. Kennedy was looking around and waving at the crowd when suddenly he lowered his head, lifted his hands, and seemed to freeze in this position. Because this bullet entered Kennedy's back and exited his throat it passed close to his spine. The pressure of the passing projectile would have damaged his central nervous system, causing these uncontrollable muscle contractions.

Investigators know that when the bullet exited Kennedy's throat it was spinning sideways. This is because the entry wound in Connally's back made by the same bullet was two inches wide. Once inside Connally, the bullet continued to tumble. It cracked one of his ribs before it exited his chest on the right. Since X-rays found lead in the wounds on Connally's wrist and left thigh, investigators know the bullet had hit these places. The reason Connally's wrist and leg were not severely damaged was because the bullet had become quite flat by now and had also slowed down significantly.

Because of the wild ride this bullet took, it was also called the "magic bullet." In reality, this bullet was far from magic and was actually behaving quite normally for a bullet of this type. These Western 6.5mm cartridges contained a solid lead bullet that was coated in copper. The copper allowed the bullets to travel at a very high speed, which allowed them to better pierce their target. Therefore, it makes sense that this bullet could go completely through two men who were lined up, and the natural tumbling of the bullet sent it zigzagging around.

## The Second Bullet Ended the President's Life

Some people question where the second shot that hit the president really came from. Because the president's head jerked backward it may seem as if he had been hit from the front. This would be in the opposite direction of the book depository. However, close examination of the Zapruder film shows that the second bullet hit the president in the back of the head. The reason his head moved backward was because of all the brain matter, bone, and blood that was exiting through the front of his head. The force of this much material leaving through the front of the head threw the skull backward. To further support this, the inside of the car's front windshield was covered with the president's blood.

## The Conclusions

Ten months after the Warren Commission was formed, Frazier and his team had reached the following conclusions:[4]

1. The shots that killed President Kennedy and wounded Governor Connally were fired from the sixth-floor window of the Texas School Book Depository.

2. Three shots were fired.

3. The bullet that went through President Kennedy's throat also wounded Governor Connally.

4. The shots that killed President Kennedy and wounded Governor Connally were fired by Lee Harvey Oswald.

5. Approximately forty-five minutes after the shooting, Oswald killed Dallas Police Patrolman J. D. Tippit with a revolver altered to shoot .38-caliber bullets.

6. A little over an hour after the shooting, Oswald resisted arrest at a movie theater and attempted to shoot one of the arresting Dallas police officers.

7. No evidence has been found that Oswald had partners in this crime.

To this day, the assassination of President Kennedy stands as one of the most emotional events in U.S. history. People alive at the time of the shooting all seem to remember where they were when they heard the news. This horrific crime also stands in the history books as a historical case in firearms identification, not only because it involved a president, but because of the thoroughness and scientific objectivity that was used in the investigation.

# HISTORIC CASES IN FIREARMS IDENTIFICATION

In 1794, a man was shot with a muzzle-loader. This gun uses a small ball of paper to secure a bullet on top of some gunpowder. At autopsy, this wad of paper was collected and found to be a piece torn from a sheet of music. Later, a suspect was arrested. He had the same sheet of music in his pocket. The torn piece from inside the dead man matched the tear in the paper found on the suspect.

The discipline of firearms identification involves examining toolmarks: small identifying marks made by tools. The earliest known toolmark comparison case involving firearms occurred in 1835 in London, England. A homeowner was shot and killed, and the servant was suspected of the crime. Henry Goddard, one of the Bow Street Runners (an early London police force), investigated the case. By thorough examination of the physical evidence, Goddard was able to identify a visible flaw in the fired bullet. At this time bullets were handmade using melted metal poured into molds. Because each mold was also handmade, each bullet was one-of-a-kind. Goddard traced the mark to the manufacturer's mold. He also identified the paper wad used as having been torn from a newspaper that was found in the servant's quarters.

One of the first times a gun "expert" testified in court was in the United States. In 1902, Judge Oliver Wendell Holmes was hearing a murder case. He asked a gunsmith if he could tell if the suspect's gun fired the murder bullet. The gunsmith test fired the gun into cotton. He used a magnifying glass and a microscope to examine the test bullets and the one from inside the dead man. In court, the gunsmith testified to the jury that the marks on the test bullets were identical to those on the crime bullet and the suspect was convicted of murder. Holmes said, "I see no other way in which the jury could have learned so intelligently how a gun barrel would have marked a lead bullet fired through it."[5]

# Exploding Bullets

"Honey, I forgot to duck." These were the words President Ronald Reagan spoke to his wife after he had survived a would-be assassin's bullet on March 30, 1981.[1] President Reagan had gone to the Washington Hilton hotel to give a speech. When leaving through a side door, he was met by a pushing crowd of reporters, tourists, and citizens hoping to catch a glimpse of him. As the waving and smiling president walked to his car, a man in a tan raincoat stepped forward and fired six shots from a handgun. In the blink of an eye, four men were hit.

Three of these men lay bleeding on the cement sidewalk outside the Washington Hilton. They would remain there until ambulances could weave their way through the confusion to help them. Press secretary James Brady had been shot in the head near his left eye. Later, Brady would be wheeled past Reagan in the hospital. Reagan was

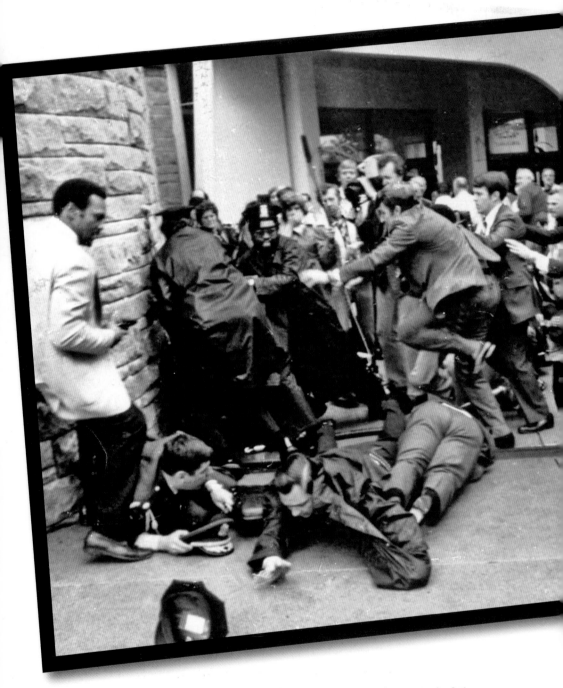

Secret Service agents try to take control of the
scene after President Reagan was shot.

told it was unlikely Brady would live. Brady did live, but he had suffered severe brain damage. Another man down was D.C. police officer Tom Delehanty. While the bullet stopped just short of his spine, Delehanty suffered permanent nerve damage in his arm. This disability forced him to retire from the police force. When the shooting started, Secret Service agent Tim McCarthy did his duty by standing spread-eagle in front of the president to shield him. Agent McCarthy was shot directly in the chest. Amazingly, he survived.

Reagan later wrote that when he was walking toward his limo, he heard what sounded like firecrackers over his left shoulder. Next he was surprised when Secret Service agent Jerry Parr suddenly grabbed him by the wrist and threw him through the open door of the limousine onto the empty seat. Agent Parr then threw himself on top of the president to shield him as he ordered the driver to head to the safety of the White House. "Jerry, get off," cried Reagan, "I think you've broken one of my ribs."[2] The pain the president felt was not a broken rib. He had been shot.

When the president began to cough bright red bubbles of blood, Agent Parr shouted to the limo driver to head to George Washington University Hospital. By the time the president arrived at the hospital, he could barely breathe and had lost a tremendous amount of blood.

The confusion that followed this shooting did not prevent the Secret Service and police from doing their duty. When the man in the raincoat stepped from the crowd, he was able to rapidly fire six shots before he was tackled by police and Secret Service agents. The officers had difficulty putting the cuffs on the shooter and were not gentle about securing this dangerous man. The officers and agents continued to hold the man down until a police cruiser could make its way into the crime scene. They picked the shooter up and carried him quickly to the closest police car only to find the door wouldn't open. Luckily, a second car had arrived and the agents and shooter piled in. Now packed in the back seat with Secret Service agents all around the shooter, the cruiser sped towards the police station with lights flashing and the siren screaming. In a jail cell the man was read his rights and searched. His name was John Hinckley, Jr., he was twenty-five years old, and he came from a wealthy family. This man had traveled to Washington, D.C., with the sole purpose of killing the president.

Agents next searched room 312 of the Park Central Hotel, which had been rented by Hinckley the day before. Books about the murder of John Lennon and serial killer Ted Bundy were found. Also found were some tapes Hinckley had made of a few awkward phone calls he had made to the famous actress Jodie Foster, who was attending Yale University. Another important find was a letter that Hinckley had written the day of the shooting in which he told Foster he was going to kill the president to get her attention and that he knew he might not survive the day. When he was eventually taken to trial he pleaded insanity.

John Hinckley, Jr. (left), pleaded insanity after attempting to kill the president.

## Finding the Bullets

While the victims were still lying on the street and the shooter was restrained against the wall of the Hilton Hotel, the Secret Service began to secure the crime scene to preserve evidence. FBI firearms investigators Gerald Wilkes and Rick Crum were two of the first agents to arrive. They found Hinckley's weapon, a .22-caliber revolver, model RG 14, serial number L731332. A videotape made at the time of the shooting recorded six shots and the gun contained six empty cartridges. The first thing Wilkes and Crum needed to do was to find those six bullets. Four bullets had hit people's bodies. A bullet hole with gunpowder residue was found on the right rear window when the presidential limo was examined, and that was called the fifth bullet. Where was the sixth?

In an effort to find the missing bullet, investigators crawled on hands and knees and finally used brooms to sweep the area. They found all kinds of trash, but no bullet. Finally, one tiny bullet hole was found in a second-story window of a building across the street from the crime scene. Bullet fragments were collected from the pavement outside the window.

## Identifying the Type of Bullet Used

It is believed that the bullet that hit the president **ricocheted** off the limo and hit him as he was being thrown into the car by a Secret Service agent. Wilkes and Crum found marks on the car that indicated the bullet had passed through the space behind the open car door and hit the frame of the car. It next flew up and struck the president under his left arm. The entry wound in the president was the shape of a small slit. This indicated the bullet had been flattened like a pancake by the time it hit him. In fact, when the bullet was extracted during surgery, it was in the shape of a flat disc and actually had paint on it that matched the limo. This Frisbee-shaped projectile had hit the president's rib and then tumbled through his lung and stopped only an inch from his heart. The lung damage is what caused the president to cough up blood and be unable to breathe.

When investigators examined the bullet taken from the president's body, they were able to make out enough rifling marks to link this bullet to those that had been test fired from Hinckley's gun. This meant that Hinckley definitely fired the bullet that hit the president. However, the bullet was so damaged that the investigators were unable to positively identify the type of bullet. The bullet that had hit press secretary James

Brady in the head was no help either, because only tiny fragments were recovered. The investigators even noted that they had rarely seen a bullet that fragmented. This observation was a hint of the surprise to come. When Wilkes and Crum received a box of ammunition that had been found in Hinckley's hotel room, they realized that some of the shooting victims were still in danger. These bullets were called "Devastators."[3] These are a type of exploding bullet that carries a tiny chemical explosive in the nose. When the bullet hits its target, the explosive in the nose detonates and causes the bullet to fragment, sending many sharp pieces of metal into the victim. This explained why the bullet inside Brady's head had been so fragmented and why the damage to his head and brain had been so severe.

## DEFORMED BULLETS CAN CONTAIN EVIDENCE

Most bullets will become deformed when they hit something hard like a wall, the sidewalk, or bone. Because of this, sometimes a bullet cannot be linked to a gun because the rifling and striation marks are not clear enough to compare. But sometimes a bullet hitting something can be a good thing for investigators. When a bullet passes through a material, it can pick up pieces of the material. Bullets have been found with microscopic bits of blood, bone, hair, dirt, brick, paint, and glass on them. Sometimes a bullet that is completely squashed can be carefully opened up in the lab and materials the bullet touched will be found inside. These can all be important clues.

A Pennsylvania police officer was charged with killing a motorist he had pulled over. The officer said that when he approached the car he tripped, his gun accidently went off, and the bullet ricocheted up and hit the victim. Unfortunately, there were no witnesses to back up his story. But the firearms and toolmarks investigators found microscopic bits of cement and glass embedded in the nose of the bullet. This evidence proved that the bullet had hit the road before it had hit the victim.

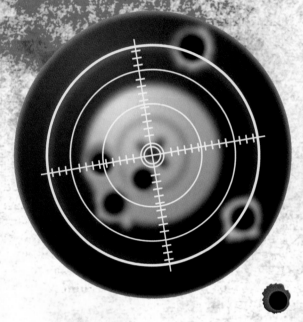

# TYPES OF BULLETS

## Bullet Shapes

The shape of a bullet influences how fast it will fly and how hard it will hit the target. There are three basic shapes: round nose, semi-wadcutter, and wad-cutter. Wadcutters are only used in revolvers.

**Round Nose**

**Semi-Wadcutter**

**Wadcutter**

## Bullet Material

Lead bullets are the oldest type of bullet material. Most lead bullets are a mixture of lead and antimony. They are inexpensive but slow. Because lead is soft, lead bullets also dirty the inside of the gun barrel. Lead bullets are most often used for target shooting and practice.

Lead bullets can be completely covered in a metal jacket (full-jacket), or partially covered (semi-jacketed or soft point). The jacket metal is usually copper. Full metal jackets fly faster and have good penetration because they do not expand. Soft points expand a little. Both types will deform when they hit a hard object.

**Full Metal Jacket**

**Semi-Jacketed
or Soft Point**

**Semi-Jacketed
Hollow Point**

## Special Bullets

A hollow-point bullet has a hollow cavity in the nose. When it hits a target it opens up, or "mushrooms." This expansion results in less penetration but more damage.

This hollow-point bullet has mushroomed.

Armor-piercing bullets are made to go through body armor. There are numerous types of these bullets. Some are made of solid brass or bronze, some have pointed tips to improve penetration, and some have a hard steel center.

Bullets can also differ in the amount of gunpowder they contain. "Maximum," "Magnum," and "Special" are all terms used to indicate that a cartridge contains extra gunpowder and is more powerful. The diameter of these cartridges is the same as the regular ones, so the caliber does not change. However, to hold the extra gunpowder the cartridge has to be longer.

## Were President Reagan and Police Officer Delehanty Still in Danger?

Once the FBI investigators understood that exploding bullets had been used, they needed to determine exactly what type of explosive charge was contained in those bullets. Many of the chemicals used in exploding bullets are poisonous. If that were the case here, then all four victims could still end up dying even though they had survived the initial shooting.

Agents were sent immediately to Norcross, Georgia, where the Devastators were made. It was learned that the explosive charge was lead azide. Even though the bullet had been removed from the president, investigators needed to know whether any of the lead azide had entered his bloodstream. To do this, they weighed the amount of lead azide in the bullet taken from the president's body and found that it was the same amount as that taken from a new Devastator shell. This meant the president was not going to be poisoned by this bullet. The question now was why the bullet hadn't exploded. Investigators decided the bullet did

not explode because it had hit the limousine before it hit the president. When the bullet hit the limo, it flattened and sealed the explosive inside. Also, these bullets need to be traveling at a very high speed in order for the charge to explode on impact. In fact, they need to be traveling at more than nine hundred feet per second. This bullet had been slowed down by hitting the car first.

The president was not poisoned by the Devastator that hit him, but there was still Officer Delehanty to worry about. The bullet that hit Delehanty had lodged close enough to his spine that the surgeons were afraid to remove it. They felt that it was safer for Delehanty to live with the bullet inside him. But that was before it was known the bullet was a Devastator. While the bullet normally needs to be traveling very fast to detonate, the lead azide charge is still very unstable. One FBI investigator found this out the hard way when he tried to take a Devastator bullet apart under a microscope. Luckily, when the bullet suddenly exploded, the microscope shielded him so he only suffered minor injuries. This event made it clear that the bullet in Delehanty could explode someday. It was also possible the lead azide could begin to leak out and poison the officer. It was no longer safe to leave the bullet inside Delehanty's body.

When Agents Wilkes and Crum tried to explain the situation to the doctors treating Officer Delehanty, they were accused of making the whole thing up so that they could obtain the bullet for evidence. The FBI finally convinced the doctors that there really was a risk that this bullet could explode. It was Delehanty who made the final decision to undergo surgery. Removing a bullet that is near someone's spine is always complicated and risky, but this surgery was even more nerve-wracking. The doctors and nurses had to keep their minds on their work while holding their breath hoping the bullet wouldn't explode. It did not, and Officer Thomas Delehanty lived to receive a hero's award for protecting the president.

# NO SUCH THING AS COP-KILLER BULLETS

The bullets that have been incorrectly named "cop-killers" are KTW bullets. The initials stand for the three people who invented them: Kopsch, Turcus, and Ward. They have a hard brass or iron core, a pointed shape, and a Teflon coating. They were designed for SWAT teams to shoot through glass and car doors. They were not made to kill police officers. They also have not been available for sale to the general public since the 1960s.

There are actually many bullets that can penetrate police body armor. This is because there is no body armor that is "bullet-proof." All body armor is only "bullet-resistant." There are different grades of armor and in the U.S., the grades are determined by the National Institute of Justice. The grades are I, II-A, II, III-A, III, and IV. The higher the grade of armor the more bullet-resistant it is. However, the more bullet-resistant the armor, the more bulky and less comfortable it is to wear. Most police officers wear grade IIIA soft armor made of Kevlar that can stop almost any handgun bullet. SWAT teams wear the highest grade called "tactical armor" or "hard armor." These armors may contain steel or titanium plates and can stop high-powered rifle bullets. Police body armor works very well because the Bureau of Alcohol, Tobacco and Firearms studied every police officer shooting between 1985 and 1994 and found that no officer had died from armor-piercing bullets.[4]

## One More Problem

While the president was being operated on, FBI agents collected all his belongings. Agent Wilkes got a surprising call two nights after the shooting. It was Tom Kelleher, the assistant director in charge of the lab.

"'You still got all of the President's stuff?' When I told him I did, he asked, 'Did you happen to get a little flat card with an orange band on it?'

"'Yeah,' I said, 'it's in my locker.'

"Kelleher breathed a sigh of relief. 'Would you get out of bed right now and go to your office, please. Two White House staffers will meet you there.'

"'Couldn't this wait till the morning?' I asked.

"'Uh, no,' he said firmly. 'That thing you stuck in your locker box is the encoding card that arms all of our nuclear warheads. You've had it for two days and they'd really like it back.'"[5]

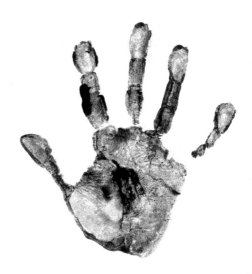

# How Serial Shootings Can Be Connected

**6**

Connecting gun crimes committed by the same weapon can be very difficult. In the 1970s, one man went on a shooting spree in New York City. It started in the summer of 1976, during America's Bicentennial. Across the country, people were celebrating the birth of the nation, but in New York City there was panic in the streets. People were afraid to be out at night because the .44-Caliber Killer was on the loose. The terror would last for over a year.

The killer first struck on July 29, 1976, at 1:00 A.M. Two teenage girls were his victims. Jody Valenti had driven her friend Donna Lauria home to the Bronx and they were talking in the car. Suddenly a man approached the passenger side door, pulled a handgun from a brown paper bag, and fired five shots into the car. The killer even continued to pull the trigger after the gun was empty. Jody leaned on the horn to call for help. Donna's father rushed outside, but it was too late for his daughter.

A bullet from a
.44-caliber Bulldog
revolver.

She died immediately from being shot in the neck. Jody was injured, but survived. Although police didn't know it, this was the first of what would be many shootings by this criminal. Over the next year, the attacker would leave six young people dead and seven more wounded.

This first shooting gave police their first real evidence, a .44-caliber bullet. New York police forensic experts examined the bullet under a microscope. The rifling marks on the bullet were very unique and they were a definite match to one particular gun, the Charter Arms Bulldog 5-shot revolver. This is how the shooter got his name: the .44-Caliber Killer.

On October 23, 1976, the killer struck a second time, again targeting two young people sitting in a car. Carl Denaro was celebrating at a local bar before he left for the Air Force. Around 2:30 A.M., Carl left the bar with his friend Rosemary Keenan. While they talked in the car outside Rosemary's home, a man approached the passenger window and fired five shots into the car. In a panic, Rosemary drove back to the bar and helped Carl inside. Both survived, but Carl had been shot in the head and part of his skull had to be replaced with a metal plate. All of the .44-caliber bullets collected from inside the car were too deformed to identify the gun that had fired them. The only thing that police could say was that a high-powered weapon was used.

The third shooting occurred on November 26, 1976. Sixteen-year-old Donna DeMasi and eighteen-year-old Joanne Lomino were walking home from the bus stop after seeing a late movie. A man began following them in the dark and then spoke to them. He acted as if he were asking for directions but then suddenly pulled a gun from his pocket and shot them. The girls were so close to Joanne's home that her father heard them screaming and rushed outside. Even though the bullet came close to hitting Donna's spine, she would be okay. Unfortunately, the bullet hit its mark in Joanne's body and shattered her spine, leaving her paralyzed for life.

# HOW TO COLLECT FIREARM EVIDENCE

When evidence is collected at a crime scene, it is photographed before it is moved. It is then placed in paper bags or containers and labeled with the initial of the collecting investigator, the date, and an exhibit number.

An investigator never picks up a handgun by putting something like a pencil inside the barrel. This may destroy identifying marks inside the barrel and compromise any fiber evidence present. The proper procedure is to first note the number and position of spent cartridge casings around the gun before it is moved. Then the investigator wears cotton gloves to pick up the gun by the grip to protect any fingerprints. No gun is ever transported loaded. For revolvers, the number of live rounds in the cylinder is counted and then the rounds are removed. For semiautomatics, the magazine is removed. Long guns are unloaded and placed in a wooden or cardboard box to be sent to the lab.

If a bullet is embedded in something like a wall, the bullet is carefully removed along with a layer of the material surrounding it so that it can also be tested. Bullets are not pulled out using tweezers, as this would make marks on the bullet. Bullets and shells are wrapped in cotton and put in non-breakable containers.

Police still didn't realize a serial killer was on the loose. The three assaults had occurred in two different city boroughs so different units were working the cases. Because no intact bullets were collected from the second and third crimes, police did not know the same weapon, a Charter Arms Bulldog, had been used.

The killer struck a fourth time on January 30, 1977, and again in Queens. Christine Freund and her fiancé John Diel were talking in their parked car when the windshield suddenly exploded. Christine was shot twice in the head. Neighbors heard the shots and called police but a few hours later Christine died at the hospital. John survived. No intact bullets were obtained from this crime scene either. This was now the third time couples sitting in cars late at night had been shot in Queens with a high caliber weapon. Detective Sergeant Joe Coffey noticed the pattern. Coffey shared his theory with Captain Joe Borrelli.

The fifth attack was on March 8, 1977. This time the killer was very bold. He attacked in broad daylight and only shot once. A young college girl named Virginia Voskerichian was walking home from class. As she approached her home, a young man walked up to her, aimed his revolver, and fired. At the last moment, Virginia held up her books in front of her for protection. The bullet was so powerful it pierced the books, hit her in the face and killed her instantly.

While the crime was horrifying, two valuable pieces of evidence were obtained. The bullet that killed Virginia was intact enough to be identified as being fired from a Charter Arms Bulldog. When it was compared to the bullet from the first shooting, the rifling marks were a match. Comparisons to bullet fragments from the other shootings also suggested the same weapon. Now the suspicions of the police were confirmed: All five attacks were connected. Second, there was an eyewitness to Virginia's murder. As the killer ran to his car, he passed a man and pleasantly said to him, "Hi mister."[1] This was the first witness to see the killer fleeing one of his crime scenes.

On March 10, police held a press conference. They said they had linked all five of the attacks to the same gun using firearms identification methods. Based on eyewitness statements, it seemed one man was acting alone. Police also had a description of the man: a white male, twenty-five to thirty years old, six feet tall, medium build, and dark curly hair.[2]

All of New York now knew there was a serial shooter on the loose and they knew what he looked like. The city was in an uproar. Because most of the victims were brunettes, women started dying their hair blond. People were not hanging out at night anymore. Citizens were screaming for the psycho to be caught. At the March 10 press conference, police announced that a special task force named Operation Omega had been assembled to catch the killer. This task force would grow from fifty to over three hundred police officers by the time the killer was caught.

Despite the task force's efforts, the killer struck a sixth time. On April 17, 1977, eighteen-year-old Valentina Suriani and her twenty-year-old boyfriend Alexander Esau sat in a parked car. At 3 A.M., a car pulled alongside them and the driver fired two shots. Valentina died instantly and Alexander died later at the hospital. This time the killer added a new twist to his crimes. At the scene, police found a letter addressed to Captain Borrelli. It was two pages of misspelled words and confusing sentences, but the hatred of the killer was obvious. It was also in this letter that the killer gave himself a new name. "I am deeply hurt by your calling me a wemon [sic] hater. I am not. But I am a monster. I am the 'Son of Sam.' I am a little brat."[3] The .44-Caliber Killer would now be known as Son of Sam.

On June 26, 1977, Son of Sam struck for the seventh time. Judy Placido and Sal Lupu were driving out of a nightclub parking lot. Judy said to Sal, "This Son of Sam is really scary, the way that guy comes out of nowhere. You never know where he'll hit next."[4] The next instant their car was sprayed with .44-caliber bullets. Neither Judy nor Sal understood at first what had happened. Sal was not hit and actually thought someone had thrown rocks at the car. As he ran back into the nightclub to get his friends, Judy looked in the car's rearview mirror. She saw that she was covered with blood. Despite being shot three times, Judy lived.

The eighth and last attack happened on July 31, 1977. Bobby Violante and Stacy Moskowitz were parked in a car when Stacy noticed a man looking at them. The man turned and disappeared behind some trees just before gunshots rang out in the dark. Even though Bobby was shot twice in the face, he was still able to see Stacy slumped against the inside of the car. Police arrived quickly and both victims were taken to the hospital. Bobby survived, but he went completely blind in one eye and partially blind in the other. Stacy's head wounds were too severe and she died at the hospital.

After Stacy and Bobby's attack, a witness came forward. Mrs. Cacilia Davis told police that when she was walking her dog that night she saw a man acting suspiciously. She returned to her house and just after closing her door, she heard what she thought were firecrackers. But when she watched the news the next morning, she knew it hadn't been firecrackers she heard. The description Davis gave police matched the one given by the man who saw Virginia Voskerichian killed. Davis also gave police a key piece of information. Many of the cars parked in that area that night had been ticketed. She noticed one in particular that was parked beside a fire hydrant, a cream-colored Ford Galaxy.

Police went through all the parking tickets and found one given to a David Berkowitz, a twenty-four-year-old postal worker. The Omega investigators had heard Berkowitz's name before. He had been writing bizarre letters to people and had even set a small fire outside a neighbor's door. When police went to Berkowitz's home they saw the cream-colored

David Berkowitz was found to be the Son of Sam killer.

Ford Galaxy parked on the street. On the back seat of his car was a Commando Mark III rifle. Because this was in plain view, the officers had the right to search the car. Inside they found a duffle bag with maps of the crime scenes and another Son of Sam letter to Captain David Borrelli that threatened more murders. The police quietly waited outside until a man left the apartment building and got in the car, then they pounced. As police swarmed the car shouting and pointing their weapons, the man in the driver's seat smiled and remained very calm.

The man had with him a brown paper bag containing a Charter Arms Bulldog revolver that was later matched to the two bullets in police evidence. In his apartment, police found a diary that not only detailed all the Son of Sam crimes, but also described how he had set over one thousand fires and stabbed several people. In addition to all of this evidence, David Berkowitz confessed to everything. But he also pled insanity later. He claimed that his neighbor's dog and various demons tormented him and only left him alone after he killed. The insanity plea did not sway the jury and Berkowitz was found guilty of murder and sentenced to 365 years in prison.

## The Beltway Snipers

In the fall of 2002, there was another string of shootings. This time, state-of-the-art computer databases helped police figure out very quickly that a serial killer was at work. For twenty-three days, a sniper terrorized the areas of Washington, D.C., Virginia, and Maryland. Ten people were dead and three were wounded. Because all types of people were shot in all types of places, everyone was scared. Even the police wore bulletproof vests while investigating the crime scenes. What was surprising was that

when the suspect was caught, there wasn't just one sniper but two working together. One of them was only seventeen years old.

On October 2 at 5:20 P.M., a cashier at a Michaels craft store felt something fly through her hair. When police investigated, they found a large caliber bullet embedded in the rear wall of the store. At 6:04 P.M., just two miles away, James Martin was shot in the back and killed as he walked through the parking lot of the Shoppers Food Warehouse. There seemed to be no motive to either shooting.

# LINKING CRIMES USING DATABASES

In the early 1990s, the FBI began development of their firearm database called **DrugFire** database, while the ATF built their own database called **Integrated Ballistic Identification System (IBIS)**. Both systems have the same goal: a computerized database containing pictures of bullets and shell casings that are collected from crime scenes. Each one takes highly detailed digital pictures of the firearms identification evidence and then organizes it in a database. Other images are fed in and a search finds "probable" matches based on caliber, number of lands, twist, and the shape of the firing pin mark. Matches are rated on a scale of 1 to 100, with 100 being the best match. These are just probable matches because a firearms examiner must still perform an actual test fire examination to be sure.

Both databases could tell investigators whether bullets or shell casings with the same markings had been collected at other crime scenes. However, there needed to be a single unified database so that all police agencies had access to the same information. In 1997, the **National Integrated Ballistic Identification Information Network (NIBIN)** was created to merge the DrugFire and IBIS databases.

Linking multiple crimes is a great help to investigators, but even better if the database can tell what gun fired those cartridges and the name of a suspect. For example, during the week of January 4, 2010, the Colorado Springs Police Department was dispatched to a home where a victim had received multiple gunshot wounds. Later that month in New York City, police arrested three men during a traffic stop and confiscated two handguns, a .40-caliber and a .45-caliber. After test firing, the bullets and shells from these guns were run through NIBIN. The .40-caliber pistol was used in the Colorado shooting. The suspect pled guilty and was sentenced to sixteen years.[5]

October 3 was total chaos. Five different people in five different places were going about their business until they suddenly collapsed. All had been shot. All were dead. The horror began at 7:41 A.M., when landscaper James L. Buchanan was shot dead while mowing the grass at a car dealership. At 8:12 A.M., part-time taxi driver Premkumar Walekar was killed while pumping gasoline. At 8:37 A.M., Sarah Ramos was shot in the head while reading a book at a bus stop. At 9:58 A.M., Lori Ann Lewis-Rivera was killed while vacuuming her minivan. At 9:15 P.M., Pascal Charlot was shot while he took a walk.

Police Chief Charles Moose of Maryland's Montegomery County headed the investigation. Chief Moose called in the FBI and ATF to help. The ATF's firearms identification laboratory was immediately valuable. The ATF lab examined the bullets, bullet fragments, and the entry and exit wounds on the victims. They then used their computer databases to determine what type of bullet had killed these people. It was a .223-caliber bullet that had killed all the victims. This type of ammo is designed to travel at a very high speed, three thousand feet per second. It is also made to expand and fragment when it hits a body. This is why no intact bullets had been found so far. The problem was that this type of ammo could be used in many different rifles, so the exact weapon being used was still unknown.

Remarkably, the ATF was able to take the earliest evidence obtained and link all the crimes. However, the police still did not know they were dealing with two serial killers working as a team. The investigation was also slowed down when false leads emerged early in the investigation that caused a lot of confusion. A number of witnesses at the different crime scenes said they saw a white box truck in the vicinity. Police used up a lot of time on these leads when they should have been looking for a beat-up 1990 blue Chevy Caprice with New Jersey license plates. Even more frustrating was that this very car was pulled over many times by police.

On October 1 and 2 alone, the car was stopped by police six times! Because the driver didn't have any arrest warrants he was always let go. Another reason this man looked innocent was because he was always in the company of a young boy. The FBI profile of the sniper described one person, not two, and not a seventeen-year-old boy.

The next two shootings gave police more valuable firearms evidence. On October 4, a woman survived being shot in a parking lot. The bullet entered her lower back and exited her left front and lodged inside her minivan. The bullet was rushed to the ATF's lab and compared to the fragments. It was official, all the shootings were connected.

On October 7, at 8:09 A.M., a thirteen-year-old boy named Iran had just been dropped off at school when he was shot. As his aunt began to drive away she saw in her mirror that he was in trouble. She rushed back, picked him up, got him to the hospital, and he survived. It was at this crime scene that police found a good shell casing. Now if police found a gun it could be matched to the intact bullet and shell casing.

Unfortunately, the killings continued. On October 9, Dean Meyers was shot in the head while pumping gas. On October 11 at 9:30 A.M., Kenneth Bridges was shot dead while pumping gas. On October 14 at 9:15 P.M., Linda Franklin was shot dead after she finished shopping at a Home Depot. On October 19 at 8:00 P.M., Jeffrey Hopper was shot in a parking lot near a Ponderosa steakhouse, but he survived. On October 22, bus driver Conrad Johnson was shot dead at 5:56 A.M. while standing on the steps of his bus.

## The Shooters Were Trying to Communicate

Near the school where Iran was shot, police found a playing card with a picture of a skeleton and "Dear policeman, I am God," handwritten on it.[6] In the woods near the Ponderosa, police found a four-page letter from the shooters in which they wrote "Your children are not safe, anywhere,

John Allen Muhammad was one of the two suspects in a sniping case in Maryland.

at any time," and also demanded 10 million dollars.[7] Handwriting experts said that the writing on the skeleton card matched that of the letter. The shooters had also been trying to speak with investigators by phone, but kept calling incorrect numbers. Because the FBI was using a database to keep track of phone calls, eventually all the taped phone calls made their way to Chief Moose's group. Without databases this probably would have never happened.

These phone calls were a big mistake for the snipers. In one of their phone calls, the snipers bragged of a shooting in Alabama. When police checked, they found out there had been two suspects in that shooting

Prosecutors examine a photo of John Allen Muhammad's car, which he had used as a sniper's nest.

and one had dropped a gun catalogue. A fingerprint had been lifted from the catalogue that matched Lee Boyd Malvo.[8] Investigators then found out that Malvo was often in the company of an older man named John Allen Muhammad. After talking with people who knew the two, police discovered that forty-one-year-old Muhammad had helped the young Malvo enter the U.S. from Jamaica illegally. Muhammad had a lot of control over Malvo, and he had taught the boy how to shoot. He had even called Malvo "Sniper" in front of other people. These two were definitely sticking out as possible suspects. When police learned that Muhammad owned a 1991 blue Chevy Caprice with New Jersey license plates, they made sure a description of this car was everywhere in the news.

On October 24, a man parked at a rest stop in Maryland called police to say he was looking at the blue Chevy Caprice that had been all over the news. The police made their way to the rest stop. It was an extremely dangerous situation. Officers used tractor trailer trucks to shut off all escape routes. They called in dog units and stationed them in the woods and across the highway in case anyone tried to run. When everything seemed secure, the SWAT teams, in full armor, approached the car. Inside were a man and boy sleeping. The car was a mess with food containers, soda cans, and dirty clothes everywhere. The two sleepy and dirty passengers were so surprised when the SWAT team pulled them out that they were easily arrested and taken away. To make sure no mistakes were made, police waited for a search warrant before touching the car. Once inside, they found that the car had been made into a sniper's nest. The back seat collapsed so that the shooter could lie down into the trunk and aim through a hole that had been cut near the license plate.

In the car was a Bushmaster XM15-E2S .223-caliber rifle. This rifle was quickly test fired and the test bullets and shells were found to match the intact bullet, the fragments, and the shell casing from the crimes. Both shooters were charged with capital murder in the state of Virginia.

The field of firearms identification has helped solve crimes for over four hundred years. As techniques continue to improve, more of the guilty criminals will be put to justice.

Muhammad was sentenced to death and executed on November 10, 2009. Since Malvo was only seventeen at the time of the crimes, he was sentenced to life without parole.

While the FBI and ATF databases helped link these crimes quickly, it may not have been soon enough. After more investigation on the Bushmaster rifle, it was discovered that these two had been killing people before the cluster of shootings in October. Possibly the first murder for this team was twenty-one-year-old Keenya Cook. She was killed by a single shot to the head while standing at her uncle's front door. This murder was in Tacoma, Washington, in February 2002.[9] While still mournful, the families of the victims of these earlier unsolved crimes are grateful to know who was responsible.

For over four hundred years, the field of firearms identification has helped to solve violent crimes. Over those years, many people have made important contributions to the field. Long ago, firearms investigators started with matching handmade bullets to the molds that made them. Today these investigators use sophisticated computer databases to keep track of guns used in crimes all over the world. Because firearms investigators are now able to identify practically any make of bullet and shell, and connect them to specific guns with a high level of accuracy, they are able to bring the guilty to justice.

## What Do Firearms Identification Experts Do?

A firearms investigator or firearms expert can have many different responsibilities. These experts may get to work in the field. Here they will carefully collect and catalog crime scene evidence such as spent shell casings, bullets, bullet fragments, and, of course, guns. Experts may also work in the laboratory analyzing the evidence that has been collected. Guns will be examined for fiber evidence and fingerprints. Guns will be test fired and microscopes used to compare crime scene evidence to the test fired bullets and shells. Acids will to be used to reveal serial numbers on guns or manufacturer's marks on shell casings. Toolmark examination will also come into play. For example, some criminals use long screwdrivers to scratch up their gun barrels in between crimes to try and prevent investigators from linking bullets to their gun. Over time a firearms expert must become familiar with the many makes of guns and ammunition that have been produced. In addition to analyzing evidence, firearms experts must give testimony in court about what evidence they found.

## What Skills Does a Firearms Expert Need?

To be a successful and reliable forensic firearms expert, a person must have certain skills.

- They must be comfortable with firearms since they will be handling and test firing them regularly.

- They must be comfortable speaking in public since an important part of their job will be giving testimony in court.

- They must write well because they will be preparing many written reports.

- They must be good in math and physics because these will be used to determine bullet trajectories and to reconstruct crime scenes.

- They must pay attention to details, be thorough and organized.

- They must have high personal integrity because this is very important work that will greatly affect other people's lives. They must report the truth no matter what their personal feelings.

- They must have good people skills because firearms will be just one part on any forensic investigation. They will be sharing evidence with other forensic departments, such as fingerprint analysis. Being a cooperative person will be an asset.

- They must have good computer skills.

## Where Do Firearms Experts Find Jobs?

Most firearms experts will find employment in crime laboratories within a city, county, or state police department. Some experts who excel at their field will be able to work for a U. S. government agency such as the Federal Bureau of Investigation (FBI), the Secret Service, the Drug Enforcement Administration, or the Bureau of Alcohol, Tobacco, Firearms and Explosives (ATF). Still other experts can find work as consultants. Consultants can work for private organizations, such as the National Rifle Association, or for lawyers who use them to verify or argue against the findings of other experts. Because crimes are committed everywhere, firearms experts are needed in every state and country.

## What Are the Hours and Pay?

According to the U. S. Department of Labor, forensic scientists in general get starting salaries of $20,000 to $40,000. With more study and experience, scientists in this field can make as much as $100,000. The number of forensic science jobs is expected to increase as forensic evidence becomes more accepted in convicting suspects. However, it has become a popular field so the competition for these jobs will also increase.[1]

## How Does Someone Become a Firearms Expert?

Police officers and other people in law enforcement can become forensic firearms experts by taking some additional training and classes. Other people will start from scratch by completing high school and then earning a college degree in forensic science or criminology. Doing an internship during college would be extremely helpful. Even after college, many firearms experts get advanced degrees like a Masters or a Ph.D.

Once someone becomes a firearms examiner, they still continue their education to keep up with the latest technology. One way to do this is to join a professional association like the Association of Firearm and Tool Mark Examiners (AFTE),[2] or the American Academy of Forensic Sciences (AAFS).[3] These professional organizations offer continuing education classes as well as a way to interact with others in this field of forensics. The sharing of knowledge and experience is necessary for a person to establish himself as a reliable professional.

# CHAPTER NOTES

## Chapter 1. War Crimes in Croatia

1. Ian Traynor, "How Sljivancanin Plotted The Vukovar Massacre," *The Guardian*, June 14, 2003, <http://www.guardian.co.uk/world/2003/jun/14/balkans.warcrimes1> (November 5, 2010); Robert Parsons, "Balkans: Vukovar Massacre Trial Begins In The Hague," *Radio Free Europe Radio Liberty*, October 11, 2005, <http://www.rferl.org/content/Article/1062028.html> (November 5, 2010).

2. William J. Fenrick, "Annex X.A Mass Graves-Ovcara near Vukovar, UNPA sector east, Final report of the United Nations Commission of Experts," Part II, December 28, 1994, <http://www.ess.uwe.ac.uk/comexpert/ANX/X-A.htm> (November 5, 2010).

3. Ovcara Case: Trial for the war crimes against the war prisoners, War Crimes Chamber of the District Court in Belgrade, Serbia.

4. Guy Gugliotta, "Police Get a New Shot at Solving Firearms Crimes," *Washington Post*, August 22, 1999, <http://articles.latimes.com/1999/aug/22/local/me-2513> (November 5, 2010).

## Chapter 2. The St. Valentine's Day Massacre

1. Jonathan Eig, *Get Capone: The Secret Plot That Captured America's Most Wanted Gangster* (New York: Simon & Schuster, Inc., 2010), p. 191.

2. Calvin H. Goddard, "The Valentine Day Massacre: A Study In Ammunition-Tracing," *The American Journal of Police Science* 1 (1930), pp. 60–78.

3. Lisa Steele, "Ballistics," in *Science for Lawyers*, ed. E. Y. Drogin (Chicago: American Bar Association Section of Science and Technology Law, 2008), p. 1.

4. Laurence Bergreen, *Capone: The Man and the Era* (New York: Simon and Schuster, Inc., 1994), pp. 312–314.

5. Eig, pp. 223–225.

6. Ibid.

## Chapter 3. Firearms Experts, Real and Fake

1. Jim Fisher, "Firearms Identification: The Stielow Firearms Identification Case," *The Jim Fisher Official Website*, <http://jimfisher.edinboro.edu/forensics/stielow.html> (November 5, 2010).

2. Edwin M. Borchard, "Stielow and Green," in *Convicting the Innocent*, (Garden City, N.Y.: Garden City Publishing, 1933), <http://library.albany.edu/preservation/brittle_bks/Borchard_Convicting/chpt39.pdf> (November 5, 2010).

3. Rob Warden, "Nelson Green: Meet the Exonerated," Northwestern Law, Bluhm Legal Clinic, Center on Wrongful Convictions, <http://www.law.northwestern.edu/wrongfulconvictions/exonerations/nyGreenSummary.html> (November 5, 2010).

4. James E Hamby and James W. Thorpe, "The History of Firearm and Toolmark Identification," *The Association of Firearm and Tool Mark Examiners Journal*, 31 (1999), <http://firearmsid.com/A_historyoffirearmsID.htm> (November 5, 2010).

5. "Strange Case of Charles F. Stielow: Governor's Actions Ends Long Controversy on Life of Man Who Was Influenced to Confess Murder," *The New York Times*, May 12, 1918, <http://query.nytimes.com/gst/abstract.html?res=9B00E7DB103BEE3 ABC4A52DFB3668383609EDE> (November 5, 2010).

6. David Fisher, *Hard Evidence: How Detectives Inside the FBI's Sci-Crime Lab Have Helped Solve America's Toughest Cases* (New York: Simon & Schuster, Inc., 1995), p. 229.

7. Lisa Steele, "Ballistics," in *Science for Lawyers*, ed. E. Y. Drogin (Chicago: American Bar Association Section of Science and Technology Law, 2008), p. 5.

8. Francis Russell, "Sacco Guilty, Vanzetti Innocent?" American Heritage, History's Homepage, <http://www.americanheritage.com/articles/magazine/ah/1962/4/1962_4_4.shtml> (November 5, 2010).

## Chapter 4. The Unpredictable Path of Bullets

1. David Fisher, *Hard Evidence: How Detectives Inside the FBI's Sci-Crime Lab Have Helped Solve America's Toughest Cases* (New York: Simon & Schuster, Inc., 1995), pp. 262–263.

2. Ibid., p. 258.

3. Newseum with Cathy Trost, Susan Bennett, *President Kennedy Has Been Shot* (Illinois: Sourcebooks Inc, 2003), p. 196.

4. *The Official Warren Commission Report On The Assassination of President John F. Kennedy* (New York: Doubleday & Company, Inc, 1964), pp. 18–21.

5. Brian Innes, *Body In Question: Exploring The Cutting Edge In Forensic Science* (New York: Barnes & Noble, 2005), p. 39.

## Chapter 5. Exploding Bullets

1. Ronald Reagan.com, *The Official Site*, "March 30, 1981," <http://www.ronaldreagan.com/march30.html> (November 5, 2010).

2. Paul Kengor, *God and Ronald Reagan: A Spiritual Life* (New York: HarperCollins Publishers, 2004), p. 184.

3. Philip Taubman, "Explosive Bullet Struck Reagan, F.B.I. Discovers," *The New York Times*, April 3, 1981, <http://www.nytimes.com/1981/04/03/us/explosive-bullet-struck-reagan-fbi-discovers.html> (November 5, 2010).

4. David Kopel, "The Return of a Legislative Legend: Debating "cop-killers.," *The National Review*, March 1, 2004, <http://old.nationalreview.com/kopel/kopel200403010926.asp> (November 5, 2010).

5. David Fisher, *Hard Evidence: How Detectives Inside the FBI's Sci-Crime Lab Have Helped Solve America's Toughest Cases* (New York: Simon & Schuster, Inc., 1995), pp. 236–237.

## Chapter 6. How Serial Shootings Can Be Connected

1. TruTV.com Crime Library, "Criminal Minds and Methods: Son of Sam," <http://www.trutv.com/library/crime/serial_killers/notorious/berkowitz/22.html> (November 5, 2010).

2. Lawrence D. Klausner, *Son of Sam* (New York: McGraw-Hill Book Company, 1981), pp. 126–127.

3. Tom Philbin and Michael Philbin, *The Killer Book of Serial Killers* (Illinois: Source Books Inc., 2009), pp. 123–124.

4. Klausner, p. 185.

5. Bureau of Alcohol, Tobacco, Firearms and Explosives, "Hits of the Week, 2010," <http://www.nibin.gov/press/releases/2010/010410-012510-hits-of-the-week.html> (November 5, 2010).

6. Angie Cannon, *23 Days Of Terror: The Compelling True Story Of The Hunt And Capture Of The Beltway Snipers* (New York: Pocket Books, 2003), p. 80.

7. Ibid., pp. 194–196.

8. Charles A. Moose and Charles Fleming, *Three Weeks In October: The Manhunt for the Serial Sniper* (New York: Penguin Group Inc., 2003), pp. 228–229.

9. Scott Calvert and Alec MacGillis, "Ballistics Tests Tie Sniper Suspects To Tacoma Killing," *The Baltimore Sun*, October 30, 2002, <http://www.dailypress.com/news/national/bal-te.md.tacoma30oct30,0,7626496.story> (November 5, 2010).

## Careers in Forensic Firearms Investigation

1. United States Department of Labor, Bureau of Labor Statistics, Occupational Outlook Quarterly, Fall 1999, "Forensic Scientists: A Career In The Crime Lab by Hall Dillon," <http://www.bls.gov/opub/ooq/1999/fall/art01.pdf> (November 8, 2010).

2. The Association of Firearm and Tool Mark Examiners (AFTE), <http://www.afte.org/AssociationInfo/a_certification.htm> (November 8, 2010).

3. American Academy of Forensic Sciences (AAFS), <http://aafs.org/about-aafs> (November 8, 2010).

# GLOSSARY

**assassination**—The murder of someone important, such as a president.

**automatic**—A gun that will continue to fire as long as the trigger is held down.

**ballistics**—The study of how a projectile moves through the air and into a target. This term is commonly, but incorrectly, used to describe firearms identification.

**breech face**—A metal surface that lies behind the cartridge in a gun.

**bullet**—The projectile that is forced out of an ammunition cartridge by exploding gunpowder.

**butt stock**—The wooden or plastic part of a long gun that is held against the shoulder when the gun is fired.

**caliber**—A measurement of a cartridge that refers to its diameter.

**cartridge**—The live ammunition that is loaded into a gun. It is made up of a bullet, gunpowder, a primer, and a metal casing. Also called a "round."

**cartridge casing**—The metal cup containing a used primer cap. This is left behind after the cartridge is fired and the bullet released. Also called a "shell casing," or just a "shell."

**comparison microscope**—A microscope that allows two bullets or shell casings to be examined simultaneously.

**cylinder**—The round part of a revolver that holds the cartridges. It revolves as cartridges are fired.

**DrugFire**—The FBI's firearms identification database.

**ejector**—A metal lip that tilts the empty shell case so that it is popped out of the gun.

**extractor**—A metal hook inside a semiautomatic handgun that pulls the empty shell case down against the ejector.

**firing pin**—A small metal pin that slams into the primer in the bottom of a cartridge, causing it to explode.

**gauge**—Measurement of a shotgun shell that indicates the number of lead balls the shell contains.

**grooves**—The cuts made into a gun barrel to rifle it.

**gunpowder**—A mixture of chemicals designed to produce a controlled explosion within the ammo cartridge.

**helixometer**—A device that allows the inside of a gun barrel to be seen.

**IBIS**—The firearms identification database created by the Bureau of Alcohol, Tobacco, Firearms and explosives (ATF).

**lands**—The raised parts created when grooves are cut into a gun barrel.

**magazine**—The container that stores cartridges in a semiautomatic or fully automatic gun.

**NIBIN**—The firearms identification database created by combining DrugFire and IBIS.

**primer**—A small metal cap in the base of a cartridge that contains explosive material.

**revolver**—A type of handgun that has a rotating cylinder that holds five or six live rounds.

**ricochet**—An object such as a bullet that bounces off a surface.

**rifle**—A type of long gun that has a rifled barrel.

**rifling**—The method of carving spiral grooves into the inside of a gun barrel so that the exiting bullet spins and flies straighter.

**semiautomatic**—A type of handgun in which live rounds are held in a magazine within the grip, allowing the gun to be reloaded quickly.

**shot**—The lead balls inside a shotgun shell.

**shotgun**—A type of long gun that does not have a rifled barrel and shoots shotgun shells instead of cartridges.

**slide**—The working part of a semiautomatic handgun that covers the barrel. When a cartridge is fired, the slide is pushed back and prepares the gun to be fired again.

**striations**—Identifying marks made on bullets and shell casings after they have been fired by a gun.

**twist**—The direction of the spiral grooves cut into a gun barrel, either clockwise or counterclockwise.

# FURTHER READING

## BOOKS

Cannon, Angie. *23 Days Of Terror: The Compelling True Story of the Hunt and Capture of the Beltway Snipers.* New York: Pocket Books, 2003.

Eig, Jonathan. *Get Capone: The Secret Plot That Captured America's Most Wanted Gangster.* New York: Simon & Schuster, Inc., 2010.

Evans, Colin. *The Casebook of Forensic Detection: How Science Solved 100 of the World's Most Baffling Crimes.* New York: John Wiley & Sons, Inc., 1996.

Innes, Brian. *Body in Question: Exploring the Cutting Edge in Forensic Science.* New York: Barnes & Noble Publishing, Inc., 2005.

Moore, Pete. *The Forensics Handbook: The Secrets of Crime Scene Investigation.* New York: Barnes & Noble Publishing, Inc., 2004.

## INTERNET ADDRESSES

**Association of Firearm and Tool Mark Examiners (AFTE).** <http://www.afte.org>.

**Bureau of Alcohol, Tobacco, Firearms and Explosives. "NIBIN: National Integrated Ballistic Information Network."** <http://www.nibin.gov>.

**The University of Utah Eccles Health Sciences Library. "Firearms Tutorial."** <http://library.med.utah.edu/WebPath/TUTORIAL/GUNS/GUNINTRO.html>.

# INDEX